LEAVE THE LIGHTS ON

How Joyful Decisions Can Save Our Species

Elizabeth Dunn and Jiaying Zhao

Atlantic Books
London

First published in the United States in 2026 by Avery, an imprint of Penguin Random House LLC, 1745 Broadway, New York, NY 10019.

First published in hardback in Great Britain in 2026 by Atlantic Books, an imprint of Atlantic Books Ltd.

Illustrations on pages 29 and 92 by Chastity Leong Ka See.

10 9 8 7 6 5 4 3 2 1

A CIP catalogue record for this book is available from the British Library.

Hardback ISBN: 978 1 80546 361 0
Trade Paperback ISBN: 978 1 80546 362 7
E-book ISBN: 978 1 80546 363 4

Printed and bound by CPI Group (UK) Ltd, Croydon CR0 4YY

Allen & Unwin
An imprint of Atlantic Books Ltd
Ormond House
26–27 Boswell Street
London
WC1N 3JZ

www.atlantic-books.co.uk

Product safety EU representative: Authorised Rep Compliance Ltd., Ground Floor, 71 Lower Baggot Street, Dublin, D02 P593, Ireland. www.arccompliance.com

Liz: To my son, Oliver Gill, whose energy and smile fills me with hope for the next generation

JZ: To my grandmother Ziqi Lu, who dedicated her life to water resource management; and my mother, Yanlin Wang, who filled my childhood with joy

LEAVE THE LIGHTS ON

'Where do joy and climate action meet? Right here in this book – as they can in our lives. The authors offer us a guide to brightening the future we all share.' **Katharine K. Wilkinson, author of *Climate Wayfinding***

'Dunn and Zhao combine rigorous research with practical wisdom to show that the most effective climate change actions are also the most personally rewarding ones – and that individual decisions can cascade into systemic change. The result is a remarkable book that is both scientifically sound and genuinely inspiring.' **Daniel H. Pink, author of *Drive*, *When*, and *The Power of Regret***

'*Leave the Lights On* is that rare book that manages to be both inspiring and practical. Dunn and Zhao bust the myth that saving the planet requires sacrifice, showing us instead that low-carbon choices can bring more happiness, not less. With crisp science, witty stories, and actionable tips, they offer a brilliant playbook for making small choices that add up to a big impact. I loved it!' **Sonja Lyubomirsky, author of *The How of Happiness***

'Be good to yourself or good to the planet? Give up driving cars and eating bacon, or do both and feel guilty about it? If you think these are your choices, you're in for quite a surprise – and quite a treat. Smart, funny, and truly illuminating, *Leave the Lights On* is grounded in cutting-edge science and filled with practical advice about how to live more joyfully *and* more sustainably at precisely the same time. Who knew that saving the world could be so much fun?' **Daniel Gilbert, author of *Stumbling on Happiness***

'Fixing climate change has often be sold as a sacrifice: if we want to have any future, we'll have to suffer today to get there. This book turns that thinking upside down. Improve your happiness and wellbeing while also reducing your carbon footprint? Many would argue that this is too good to be true; Dunn and Zhao expertly show us that it is not.' **Hannah Ritchie, author of *Not the End of the World***

'Dunn and Zhao show that there are plenty of ways to find joy while tackling climate change. With actionable tips to uplevel happiness and have an impact through low-carbon treats, investments, vacations, and much more, *Leave the Lights On* is a must read. This book will help people make smarter, happier choices – and stick with them.' **Annie Duke, author of *Thinking in Bets***

CONTENTS

LEAVE
THE
LIGHTS
ON

Happiness Is Our Best Weapon

On a sunny autumn day, Liz was biking to her research lab, which is dedicated to the study of happiness. She had been feeling increasingly preoccupied with climate change, and started wondering if she should have devoted her career to this existential threat instead. And then it hit her. She had chosen to bike to work because getting fresh air and exercise put her in a good mood. She hadn't given a second thought to the carbon she was saving. Liz realized that many everyday choices have the potential to enhance happiness and address climate change at the same time.

When she got to work, she made a beeline for her colleague: one of the world's leading sustainability scientists, Jiaying Zhao. At that moment, JZ was busy devising the perfect composting bins to get people to stop tossing their banana peels in the trash.

Liz started talking a mile a minute, explaining her idea: Together, the two of them could find "sweet spots" that would make the fight against climate change feel good. JZ realized that she had never given a second thought to happiness. But as Liz spoke, it dawned on JZ that happiness might be the missing tool for tackling climate change.

At first glance, we might seem like an odd pair. During the holiday season, JZ fields questions from the media about the carbon costs of Christmas, while Liz gets interviewed about how to have fun at parties. But after years of making a name for ourselves in wildly disparate fields, we discovered how much more we could accomplish together.

Over the past few years, our collaboration has revolutionized our thinking. For one thing, while climate change can be a polarizing issue, the desire for happiness is universal. Around the world, people google "how to be happy" more frequently than "how to get rich"—and an order of magnitude more than "how to solve climate change."

Not only that, but when many people think about climate change, they feel a sense of doom. In a global survey of ten thousand young people, 75 percent said they were frightened about the future.[1] Others protect themselves from the terror of a warming planet by ignoring the issue. After all, climate change is demoralizing. But it doesn't have to be.

New research suggests that fighting climate change and finding happiness might go hand in hand. In an experiment at the University of North Carolina, students were randomly assigned to "do three good things for the planet," like walking instead of driving, eating a plant-based meal, and reducing their energy use.[2] Other students were told to do three good things for themselves, like taking a hot bubble bath, spending time on a hobby, and ordering their favorite meal. Meanwhile, a control group of students simply kept track of their activities, without changing them. Compared to those who stuck to their usual routines, students who went out of their way to do positive things for the planet reported feeling happier that day. In fact, the results suggested that engaging in pro-environmental behaviors like walking boosted mood as much as conventional self-care activities like taking a hot bubble bath.

And it turns out that even people who don't hold strong environmental values exhibit mood benefits from engaging in environmentally friendly behaviors. In nationally representative samples, adults in the US and the UK report elevated levels of happiness when they engage in pro-environmental behaviors.[3] These emotional boosts seem to stem in part from the recognition that they are doing something helpful for society that aligns with their own values, but this isn't the whole story. Apart from helping society, actions like biking, carpooling, and cooking a plant-based meal can satisfy people's personal needs to feel competent, connected, and in control of their own choices.

Of course, not every pro-environmental behavior feels good to everybody, all the time. One of the main goals of this book is to help you identify your own personal sweet spots: changes you could make in your everyday life to cut carbon and get happier, too.

By making changes that support—rather than sacrifice—your

own personal happiness, you're more likely to stick with these changes over the long term. After all, pleasure is the most basic form of positive reinforcement. But this isn't always obvious to people, as sustainability expert Kathy Kuntz discovered in the many years she's spent trying to change people's behavior. As Kathy put it, "There's something weird about us human beings: When we think about little kids and puppies, we totally understand positive reinforcement. When we think about other adults, we want to shame them and punish them for what they're doing wrong."

The Power of Positive Emotions

Shame, guilt, fear, and anxiety have taken center stage in climate communication. Recently, the World Economic Forum put out a press release with the headline "Climate Crisis May Cause 14.5 Million Deaths by 2050." Even *Vogue* got in on the climate doom and gloom with a story titled "Clothes for the 'Apocalypse': How to Design for a Climate Crisis."

At first glance, it looks like freaking people out might be a good idea. A survey of approximately one thousand adults in the US found that individuals who reported feeling anxious about climate change were more likely to say that they were taking action on this issue.[4] But this is just a correlation, not necessarily cause and effect. For example, another survey found that people who have sex more often earn more money.[5] This doesn't mean that if you start having sex more frequently, you'll get a raise. It could just be that healthier people get more action and also do better on the job market. If we really want to know whether sexual activity leads to wealth, we could flip a bunch of coins and randomly assign some people to double their frequency of sexual intercourse. And we can apply the same type of experimental strategy to understand what kinds of messages make people want to take action on climate.

JZ teamed up with hundreds of collaborators around the world to do exactly this.[6] The team recruited more than fifty-nine thousand adults from sixty-three countries and randomly assigned them to one of many interventions that had been crafted by experts to increase climate action. One of the interventions involved exposing participants to facts about climate change that were framed in a doom-and-gloom style, drawn from real-world media sources. This doom-and-gloom approach produced one clear benefit: Participants were more likely to say they would share information about climate change on social media afterward. But the intervention backfired when it came to taking more effortful action. The researchers gave all participants the option to volunteer some of their time and energy in exchange for a donation to a tree-planting organization. Many participants volunteered, and approximately 330,000 trees were planted as a result, but participants who had been exposed to the doom-and-gloom message were less likely to donate their time. In fact, they volunteered less of their time than participants in a control group, who hadn't read any messages about climate change at all.

The researchers also asked government officials, climate

communicators, academics, and members of the public to predict how well each intervention would work. All four groups overestimated the effectiveness of the doom-and-gloom message. So, it's easy to see why people who care about climate change often frame their messages in ways that inspire fear and anxiety.

By doing so, however, we miss out on the power of positive emotions. When people feel happy, they are more likely to find novel, creative solutions to everyday problems. For example, in a series of experiments, participants watched a funny movie or received a decorative bag of candy, temporarily boosting their mood.[7] Then, they completed a creativity task, like thinking of a word that was related to three other seemingly disconnected words (e.g., *playing, credit, report*; see the footnote for the answer).[*] Compared to people in a neutral mood, those in a happy mood were better at seeing the hidden connection.

Happy people may also be more likely to vote. As part of the American National Election Study, approximately thirteen hundred US citizens were asked, "In general, how satisfying do you find the way you're spending your life these days? Would you call it completely satisfying, pretty satisfying, or not very satisfying?"[8] Surprisingly, the happiest citizens were most likely to vote. Of course, this is just a correlation, but it did hold up when the researchers controlled for other important factors, like age, race, and education. In fact, while education is one of the best predictors of voting, life satisfaction appeared to matter just as

---

[*] Answer: card

much. And studies have found similar evidence that happiness predicts voting in countries around the world—even in local village elections in rural China.[9]

Still, it's true that negative emotions can sometimes motivate action—especially quick, decisive moves. So, it's no wonder that climate activists like Greta Thunberg have had success likening our planet to a house on fire. Over time, though, this approach can get exhausting.

This has been a key takeaway for Anirudh Tiwathia, who leads research for Rare's Entertainment Lab, which supports entertainment writers to effectively embed climate content in TV and movies. When we think of Hollywood's take on climate change, the apocalyptic film *The Day After Tomorrow* springs to mind. Entertainment writers used to follow this doom-and-gloom approach, although that is changing in recent years. Anirudh thinks every kind of story has its place. But, he says, "This is a long fight. And you can't sustain a long fight while living in terror."

Decades of psychological research back him up. When people are faced with stressors, positive emotions play a key role in promoting resilience. In a classic experiment, Barbara Fredrickson and her colleagues invited university students into the lab.[10] She asked them to do something that many people fear more than death: give a speech. Then, just before the speech was set to begin, she let them off the hook, and showed them a video instead while tracking their cardiovascular recovery. Some participants saw a video of waves breaking on the beach, eliciting contentment, while others watched an amusing video of a puppy playing with a flower. Participants who watched these videos recovered faster, with their heart rates and blood pressure returning to normal more quickly, compared with those who watched a sad or neutral video. This experiment provided evidence for the *undoing hypothesis*, the idea that positive emotions can undo the potentially harmful effects of negative emotions on the brain and body.

Ed Maibach, one of the world's most influential scientists working on climate change, told us about the intense negative emotions he experienced early in his career. "For the first three years or so, I would wake up in the middle of the night in a cold sweat, pretty much every night," he said. But, over time, he learned that he couldn't let these negative emotions seep into every corner of his life. When we spoke to him, he exuded joy and energy, which he cultivates by appreciating the people who surround him. "My colleagues, my students, the allies in this work, all of them are so remarkable," he said—before fact-checking himself (as good scientists do). "Okay, not *all* of them; that's an overstatement. But so many of them are remarkable. You'd be lucky to have one or two of them in your life, and I have dozens of them." These warm feelings have been essential for keeping him in the fight—and he's been at it for more than eighteen years now.

So, even the scientists who study climate change need to cultivate feelings of joy and lightness. Similarly, while Anirudh appreciates the value of heart-wrenching movies and TV shows, he points to the benefits of embedding climate messages in more positive, lighthearted entertainment. For example, in *And Just*

Like That . . . , the sequel to the classic rom-com series *Sex and the City*, Miranda, one of the show's main characters, orders steak tacos at Chipotle. But then she changes her order to "one of those plant-based things." Anirudh and his colleagues found that after seeing Miranda switch her order, TV viewers were more likely to perceive ordering plant-based food as beneficial and trendy.[11]

Now Anirudh's team is testing the value of displaying solar panels on homes that are depicted in popular TV shows. Rather than scaring people about the devastating effects of climate change, this approach enables people to visualize an attractive and concrete solution. "All long fights have to be fundamentally grounded in an optimistic aspiration for a better future," he told us.

To make it easier for people to envision an optimistic future, researchers used AI to alter current Google Street View images of Austin, Texas, and other cities. They showed American adults what these communities would look like in the future if they passed bills prioritizing public transit, walking, and biking over driving.[12] After seeing these images, people were 20 percent more likely to support these climate-friendly policies—and this boost was even bigger among Republicans.

Studies like this one make the case that it's worth helping people see how pro-environmental choices can make everyday life better. This idea resonates with Amy Aquino, a climate activist who describes herself as a "moderately famous actress." Despite her love of acting, Amy chose to pursue a biology degree at Harvard because, as she put it, "making a living as an actress—statistically speaking—is impossible." Defying these odds, she earned roles in classics like *Working Girl* and *ER*. More recently, she combined her knowledge of science with her skill in front of the camera, creating Instagram reels tackling climate change. "When the pandemic hit, I saw all these people going out to the grocery store, and they were hoarding toilet paper and paper towels," she told us. "And toilet paper I can kind of understand. But the paper towels?! I was just genuinely confused." So, she made a funny, engaging Instagram reel introducing her followers to an amazing product: cloth towels!

Her lighthearted approach caught on, and since then she's produced many more reels highlighting what she calls "baby steps to green." Amy told us that she believes in the value of *showing* rather than telling. But, she said, most sustainability organizations "do so much telling, telling, telling. And the only people they're going to reach are those who are already convinced—because they're the only people following them."

Sustainability organizations often tell people to drive less, fly less, eat less meat, and even shower less. Less, less, less! But our research suggests that this approach is counterproductive. In a study of more than seven hundred adults in the US, we found that people were willing to engage in climate-friendly behaviors when we flipped the script and turned *less* into *more*. For example, people reported greater enthusiasm for eating more plant-based food versus less meat, and for choosing more reusable products versus fewer single-use products.

Amy's Instagram feed exemplifies this approach. Rather

than telling people what not to do, she showcases positive choices that make life better. "The more fun it is, the better," she told us. "The less judgy it is, the more people respond."

Do Individual Actions Matter?

If you find yourself at a cocktail party surrounded by climate activists and you want to stir things up, ask them whether individual actions matter in the fight against climate change. You may hear from someone like United Nations adviser Sophia Kianni, who argues, "Individual action is a distraction—shifting blame from large corporations to the average consumers."

Indeed, there are good historical reasons for her skepticism about individual action. In 2004, the world was introduced to the first "carbon footprint calculator." Although it might sound like the brainchild of an environmental organization, it was actually created by British Petroleum (BP), one of the world's largest oil and gas companies. By placing the focus on individual consumers and their personal carbon footprints, BP sought to shift scrutiny from its own outsize contribution to climate change.

BP's strategy has left a lasting legacy. The term *carbon footprint* is embedded in our cultural consciousness. And many environmental activists have concluded that even talking about individual change could inhibit system change. But here's the thing: Systems are made up of individuals. And when it comes to fighting climate change, we need action at every level. For example, to promote biking, city governments need to build safe, dedicated bike lanes—and individuals need to use those bike lanes.

It's tempting to assume that if governments and corporations build what's needed, individuals will just come along for the ride. This assumption can have devastating consequences, however, as Francis Collins discovered during his time as director of the National Institutes of Health (NIH). While running the NIH during the pandemic, Dr. Collins helped to oversee one of the greatest scientific triumphs in human history: the lightning-speed development and deployment of COVID-19 vaccines. But when asked about his biggest regrets, he explained that the NIH had focused too much on large-scale technology and not enough on individual psychology. At the end of 2021, Collins said, "I never imagined a year ago, when those vaccines were just proving to be fantastically safe and effective, that we would still have 60 million people who had not taken advantage of them."[13]

The climate movement faces a similar challenge. At a lunch we attended in April 2023, Al Gore pronounced, "We have all the technology we need to reduce emissions." But technology isn't enough. We need individuals to adopt and use the technology.

This important message is lurking behind a lot of jargon in an authoritative report from the Intergovernmental Panel on Climate Change (IPCC).[14] As the IPCC put it, "The indicative potential of demand-side strategies to reduce emissions of direct and indirect CO_2 and non-CO_2 GHG emissions . . . is 40–70% globally by 2050 (*high confidence*)." In other words, individual behavior change can reduce global emissions by 40 to 70 percent.

So, individual change is not in opposition to system change; it's our most powerful engine for system change.

Math Is Better Than Moralizing

When Liz was in her twenties, she shared a house with her boyfriend Chris. He was a passionate advocate of sustainable behavior, which Liz deeply respected. But it also made him hard to live with. When Liz would wander out of a room without turning off the lights, Chris would shoot her a withering look that said, "Why do you hate the earth?"

In Chris's defense, it's not crazy to frame climate change as a moral issue. After all, the survival of our species is on the line. But shaming others may backfire. For one thing, taking the moral high ground doesn't leave a lot of room for nuance. After all, if a behavior is morally wrong, then engaging in the behavior—even occasionally—could mean you're a bad person.

As a leader of one of the most influential environmental organizations in the world, Tamara Toles O'Laughlin saw this pattern up close. "Climate activists can shame each other for not composting or not using a metal straw," she said. "It can get dirty quick." Straws don't really matter when it comes to climate change (as we discuss in chapter 3), but relentlessly striving for the moral high ground may spur people to focus on symbolic actions—without stopping to question their real impact. And trying to be perfect all the time is exhausting. Aiming for an impossible moral standard, what Tamara calls "perverse perfectionism," leaves no room for error, and she has seen it contribute to feelings of burnout among climate activists.

Many of us are susceptible to investing our limited energy into symbolic actions, rather than trying to figure out what actions would truly have the biggest impact. Each year on a Saturday night in March, millions of people around the world turn off their lights from eight thirty to nine thirty p.m. during "Earth Hour." But while those who dutifully turn off their lights may believe they're sacrificing their Saturday night to save energy, the event organizers acknowledge that the action is purely symbolic. In our home province of British Columbia, the electric company found that the energy savings from Earth Hour was effectively zero.

It turns out that if Liz left all the lights on in her two-bedroom condo for the rest of her life, the carbon cost would be equivalent to eating thirteen hamburgers. So, Chris's withering looks were misplaced. Chris and others who genuinely care about climate change may focus on the wrong behaviors—exhausting themselves and alienating their loved ones in the process—because it can be hard to know what actions really matter.

Indeed, JZ's research suggests that people's intuitions in this area are wildly inaccurate. She and her colleagues designed a "carbon quiz," with four questions asking people to estimate the impact of pro-environmental lifestyle changes. Try the quiz before reading further.[15]

Q1. Someone takes a trip that requires driving a hundred miles in a standard, midsize car. If they switch from a standard, midsize car to a midsize hybrid car, how many miles can they now drive while still producing the same amount of greenhouse gases as they did on their trip in the standard car? Please give your best guess.

Q2. Eating meat and flying in a plane both result in greenhouse gas emissions. A person taking a one-way, economy flight from New York to London might try and make up for their emissions by giving up quarter-pound hamburgers. How many quarter-pound hamburgers would they need to give up to offset this flight? Please give your best guess.

Q3. Hang-drying clothing instead of using a dryer saves electricity, which reduces greenhouse gas emissions. If someone chooses to hang-dry one load of laundry, how long can they leave an LED light bulb switched on and still produce the same amount of greenhouse gases as if they had used the dryer? Please give your best guess.

Q4. Someone decides to reduce greenhouse gas emissions by switching to a vegetarian diet for one year. Another

> person tries to save the same amount of greenhouse
> gases by purchasing only unpackaged foods. How long
> would it take for the second person to save the same
> amount of greenhouse gases as the first one? Please
> give your best guess.
>
> Answers are in the footnote.[**]

When 965 adults in the US and Canada took this quiz, only one of them aced it. And people who were very concerned about climate change didn't do any better than others who cared less about this issue. Many thought that reducing food packaging would have roughly the same impact as going vegetarian. But, in reality, switching to a vegetarian diet would have ten times the impact on carbon emissions. In another study, people were asked to identify the single most effective action they could take to reduce emissions. One of the top responses was recycling—which, sure, is a nice thing to do. But, it has a modest impact relative to other actions, like choosing green energy, which almost no one mentioned.

Unfortunately, while the internet abounds with suggestions for how individuals can reduce their carbon footprints, these listicles rarely quantify how much of a difference each change

---

[**] The range of correct answers: Q1: 112–190 miles; Q2: 146–410 burgers; Q3: 272–354 hours; Q4: 10–12 years.

would make. And when the changes are quantified, they are typically expressed in tons of carbon. Try to picture a ton of carbon dioxide. This isn't easy. After all, carbon dioxide is an invisible gas.

In this book, we will provide you with simple, concrete diagrams that help you visualize the relative impact of various changes you could make—so you can identify where your biggest opportunities lie. And while there are many types of greenhouse gases, we will translate them all into the common currency of carbon dioxide (or carbon for short). JZ's friends nicknamed her "the human carbon calculator," so she'll make sure you know exactly how much of a difference your own choices can make. And Liz is here to ensure that you decarbonize your daily life in ways that actually make you happier. Together, we will take a tour through every major domain of life, and we invite you to explore each one with us in turn, or to jump straight to the areas that are of most interest to you (and perhaps return to the others later):

- **Eating (chapter 2):** Eating is one of life's great pleasures. An effective way to combat climate change is to go vegan, but vegans can't save the world alone. So, this chapter delivers impactful, practical, and science-based principles to reduce carbon while maximizing the pleasure of food. First, it's important to recognize that not all protein is created equal in terms of carbon emissions. For example, pound for pound, chicken has half the impact of cheese. And a BLT has a smaller footprint than a Beyond Meat burger. But where does this leave steak, lamb, and other delicious but high-carbon foods? We will show how eating these foods less often can actually renew our capacity to appreciate them. And we'll describe new research showing that eating some low-carbon foods can increase happiness. This chapter won't tell you exactly what to eat, in part because food is deeply interwoven with culture and identity. Instead, we'll give you a framework for navigating food choices—as well as some practical strategies for making new eating habits stick.

- **Spending, saving, and donating money (chapter 3):** Shopping ranks among the least happy activities in a typical day. And the fashion industry generates twice the global emissions of all flights and shipping combined. So, our shopping habits deserve a rethink. Like proteins, some types of clothing generate heftier emissions; jeans top the list at seventy-three pounds of carbon, while the average shirt generates only fourteen pounds. We'll show how cutting back on some types of spending can increase the pleasure you get from your money. And we'll highlight the best investments in low-carbon happiness, from solar panels to retirement funds and charitable donations.

- **Working and commuting (chapter 4):** Research suggests that ditching a forty-minute commute could provide emotional benefits akin to finding a romantic partner. And driving accounts for the largest share of the average American's carbon emissions. Meanwhile, many people are navigating complex decisions about whether to work from home. We'll break down the latest research and identify some key sweet spots for cutting back on commuting while reaping the benefits of time with colleagues. And for those who have to show up at the office, we'll explore how decarbonizing your commute can turn the most miserable moments of the day into some of the best.

- **Vacation (chapter 5):** Devotees of happiness research have come to value experiences over things. How can we enjoy leisure time and vacation travel—a major source of pleasurable experiences—while still minimizing emissions? We'll map out several complementary routes to dealing with this carbon conundrum. For example, instead of packing a hefty suitcase for a Paris vacation, bringing only a "capsule wardrobe" of essential, interchangeable clothing in a light carry-on can save unpleasant time at the airport while substantially reducing carbon. In fact, a typical checked bag is equivalent to bringing an extra six-year-old child along with you. We'll also tackle carbon offsets, which promise a way to travel the world without the climate guilt. Unfortunately, they are often a sham, so we'll help you find a more effective—and joyful—strategy for offsetting your travel.

- **Major life decisions (chapter 6):** In this penultimate chapter, we'll turn to the kinds of big questions that young people often wish to dodge during Thanksgiving dinner: What career will you pursue? Where will you call home? Are you going to start a family? You may have heard that having kids is the worst thing you can do for the climate. But we'll introduce you to the scientist behind this idea—who happens to be one of JZ's former students—and we'll show that bringing a new life into the world doesn't mean you're killing the planet. What may matter more is where you choose to live. For example, in Vermont, you can run an air conditioner for a week and only emit eight pounds of carbon—the weight of a newborn baby—while in Wyoming, the same air conditioner would emit 1,078 pounds, akin to a full-grown horse. So, you don't have to suffer through summer without AC if you choose to live somewhere with low-carbon energy. And you can effectively tackle climate change by pursuing a surprisingly wide variety of careers. You'll meet the chief of product for a major clothing company, a data scientist at Uber, and an "eco-surgeon," all of whom have made an outsize impact—and found joy in their careers, too.

- **Changing the system (chapter 7):** Human behavior is contagious. And approaching climate change from a place of joy can make you especially contagious. We'll show how your individual actions can have ripple effects: Whether you install solar panels, bike to work, or choose chicken over steak at a restaurant, you are influencing others more than you know. And as growing numbers of individuals adopt these behaviors, research suggests that support for pro-climate policies is likely to grow, too. By introducing you to mayors and activists, we'll give you an insider's guide to changing the system. Think of yourself as Patient (Net) Zero.

Onward

In the introduction to one of their flagship reports, the Intergovernmental Panel on Climate Change concludes with the words *Every choice matters*.[16] We appreciate this sentiment. But it also feels like a lot of pressure. And the truth is, we don't have full control over all our choices anyway. In particular, folks who can barely afford to feed their families should never feel guilty about prioritizing the financial cost of food over its carbon cost.

The more privilege you've got, though, the more room you probably have to cut back on carbon. Around the world, the top 10 percent of income earners are responsible for nearly 50 percent of emissions.[17] And if you're making $50,000 or more, you're in the top 10 percent of earners globally.[18]

Even leaving money aside, we all have limited time and bandwidth. Yes, ensuring a livable planet for our children is important—but on a typical Tuesday night, so is making sure they finish their homework and get to basketball practice. So, recognizing that you probably don't have infinite time, money, and energy, we will help you identify feasible and joyful changes that will make a real difference, rather than a purely symbolic one.

Ready to get happier?

Let's do this.

CHAPTER 2

In Defense of Bacon

Just be vegan. Done. You're welcome.

This is the message some people have taken from the climate movement. And it's not completely wrong. By going vegan, you could save around a ton of carbon each year.[1]

But many people struggle to stick with a vegan diet, especially if it involves giving up food they love.[2] The American comedian Jon Stewart reckoned with this dilemma. As he put it, "On the one side, eating mindfully and vegan seems to be the solution to nutrition, to health, to global warming. On the other side, corned beef."[3]

While giving up corned beef may be an unusual bugbear, it's common to struggle with forgoing all animal products. Juaquin James Malphurs—a rapper from Atlanta who is known professionally as Waka Flocka Flame—adopted a vegan diet, but later "dropped the vegan card." He explained, "When I started reading that vegans can't eat honey, I was like, y'all going too far. Let me fall back."[4]

Whether it's warranted or not, the perception that vegan diets are too restrictive may help to explain why less than 1 percent of the US population is vegan.[5] And from Finland to the Philippines, this number rarely tops 2 percent.[6] So, vegans can't save the world alone.

The good news is that they don't have to. Making more surgical changes in our eating habits can save a lot of carbon, while preserving—or even enhancing—the pleasure that food provides. In the pages that follow, we offer several complementary strategies for minimizing carbon while maximizing enjoyment of food.

Relish the Nuance

One important upside of vegan and vegetarian diets is that it's relatively simple to draw a line in the sand, identifying what foods you can and can't eat. Liz's husband, Michael, drew this line on a recent surfing trip with friends. Because of his concern about climate change, Michael had been moving toward an increasingly plant-based diet. But he decided that he was strictly vegetarian after a sunset surf session. While he had been out surfing, his friends had spent the evening making sheet-pan chicken with jammy tomatoes and pancetta. When he was offered a plate of chicken, he demurred. He scavenged through the fridge and ended up with cheese and crackers, leaving his friends mildly annoyed.

So, he was surprised when he later learned that chicken is a relatively low-carbon food. In terms of carbon, cheese costs more than twice as much as chicken.[7] The impact of white meats like chicken pales in comparison to red meats, such as beef and lamb. A single hamburger produces more than thirty pounds of carbon, whereas a chicken burger of the same size produces less than five pounds—the same as a Beyond Meat burger.

Pork is technically a red meat, but in the 1980s, it was re-branded in a potent American ad campaign as "the other white meat," leading to a spike in sales.[8] When it comes to carbon, pork does look more like a white meat. It has a relatively low carbon footprint, which is good news for bacon (one of Liz's favorite foods). In fact, a BLT produces less carbon than a Beyond Meat burger. As you can see with a brief glance at the figure that follows, not all animal products are created equal. This means that you don't have to give up meat to cut carbon. Just eating chicken and pork instead of beef makes almost as big a difference as becoming vegetarian.

While animal products vary dramatically from one to another, plants are almost uniformly low in terms of carbon emissions. You'll be keeping your carbon footprint low whether you choose broccoli or bok choy, apples or oranges, leeks or potatoes. Sure, you can find blogs with headlines like, "When It Comes to Sustainability, Not All Nuts Are Created Equal."[9] But

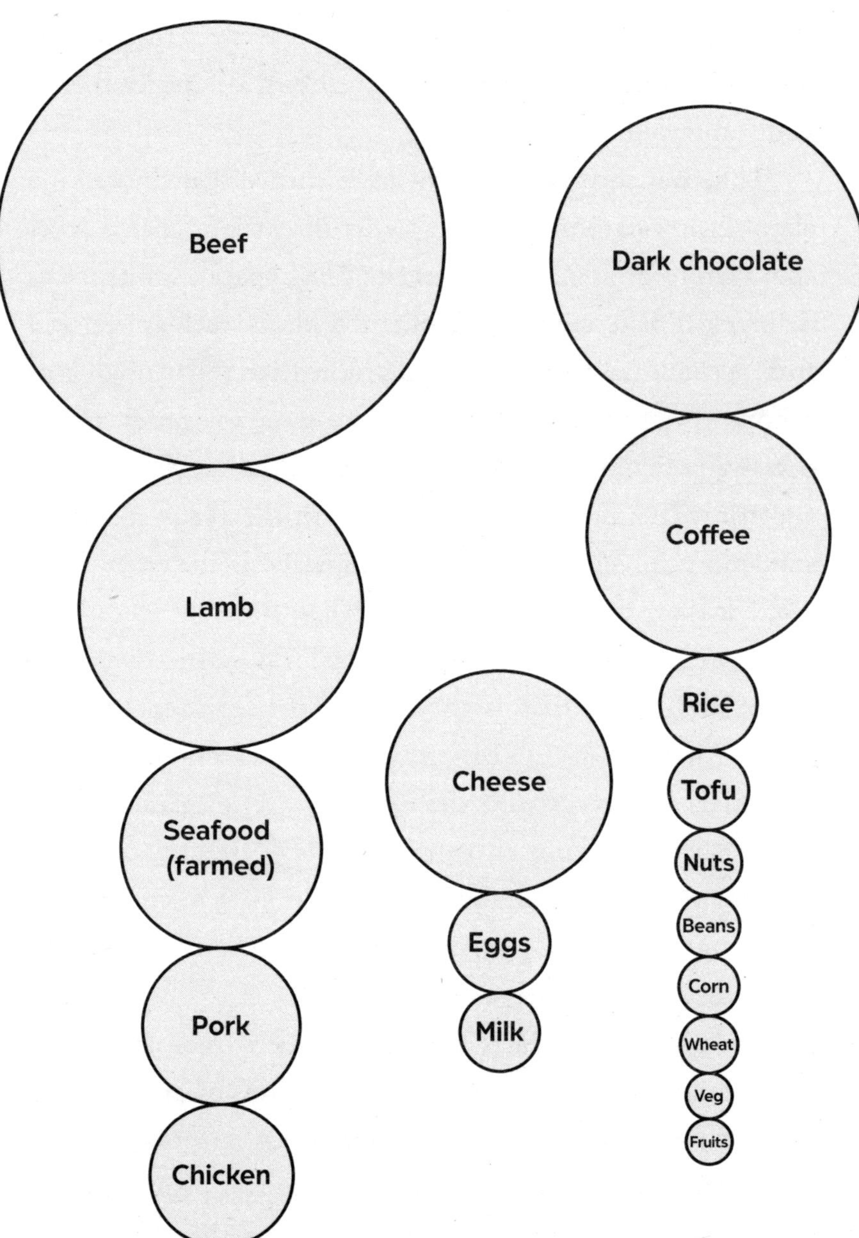

The size of each circle represents the carbon emission of each food per pound. Adapted from Poore & Nemecek (2018).[10]

the differences are so small that contemplating the carbon consequences of cashews versus peanuts probably isn't a good use of your time.

That said, as Canadians, we are legally obligated to tell you about the special benefits of maple syrup—which is a literal sweet spot for promoting pleasure and fighting climate change. This delicious bronze elixir is one of the only *carbon-negative* foods. In Quebec, maple forests capture over ten times more carbon than syrup production emits.[11] So, more syrup means less carbon. In fact, just using a teaspoon of maple syrup rather than another sweetener each day for a year would put one more maple tree into production. For those who prefer savory over sweet, seaweed is another delicious carbon-negative food: Every pound of seaweed you eat removes three pounds of carbon.[12]

To help people understand the carbon impact of their food choices, JZ's lab at the University of British Columbia teamed up with the largest dining hall on our campus, called Open Kitchen, which serves more than forty thousand meals per month. JZ's team calculated the carbon impact of each dish served by Open Kitchen, and then the dining hall added simple carbon labels on their menus, inspired by traffic lights.[13] The highest-carbon dishes, such as the Philly cheesesteak and Korean short rib, got a red label. Meanwhile, dishes that carried a modest carbon impact got a yellow label; this category included meals like chorizo penne, butter chicken, and pork belly bao. Finally, a green label was slapped on the lowest-carbon dishes, including tofu jambalaya and a curried chickpea bowl.

The dining hall kept detailed records of every purchase

made before and after the labels were introduced. When JZ and her students dug into the data, they saw that adding the green labels hadn't made much of a difference. But helping people distinguish between the red, high-carbon meals and more moderate yellow ones had a substantial impact on their choices. After the labels were introduced, people were less likely to choose the short ribs and other red meals than they had been before—and more likely to choose butter chicken and other yellow meals. In the UK, another team of researchers implemented similar labels in five dining halls at the University of Cambridge and found exactly the same pattern.[14]

It's increasingly common to see restaurant menus with green symbols indicating vegetarian options. But these new dining hall studies suggest that green labels might not have much of an impact. Instead, helping people distinguish between high-carbon meals (like short ribs) and moderate-carbon meals (like pork belly) appears to be more effective in changing choices.

And there seems to be a real appetite for this kind of labeling. When JZ's team showed people across campus the labels used at Open Kitchen, 83 percent said they would like to see the same labels in all restaurants on campus. Since then, UBC has implemented versions of these labels in all dining halls.[15] Someday, we hope similar labels will be everywhere, like nutrition information.

In the meantime, check out the figure on the next page to help you choose more carbon-friendly meals on the fly. And as you can see, most drinks pack a pretty low carbon punch—though drinking a shot of gin has the lowest carbon impact of all. Cheers!

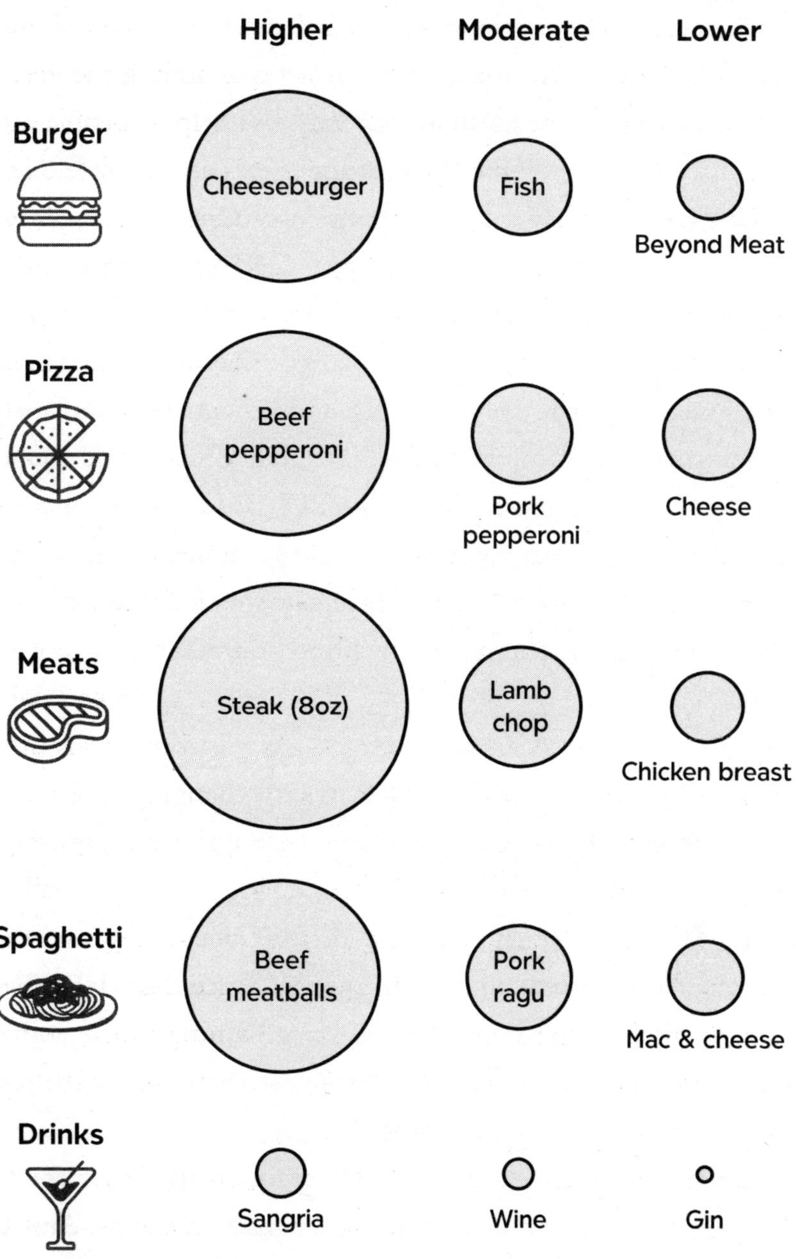

The size of each circle represents the carbon emission of each dish.

We relish the nuance of knowing that spaghetti with meatballs (one of Liz's favorite family meals) is a fairly low-carbon option, as long as the meatballs are made with pork rather than beef. But if beef is the bad boy of the meat world, where does this leave Jon Stewart and his beloved corned beef? While struggling to become vegan, he recognized that he could find some kind of fake-meat substitute for it—but the experience of eating real corned beef was about more than just the salty goodness of cured meat. Indeed, the foods we eat are often entangled with important issues of culture and identity, embedded in our memories of the past and our sense of self. Or, as Jon Stewart put it, "If I were to get fake meat, will an old Jewish man yell at me while I eat it? That's the corned beef experience I'll miss."[16] So, how can we make space for corned beef and other high-carbon foods?

Make Meat a Treat

As professors, we've encountered lots of students who are depressed about climate change. So, we've designed a Happy Climate workshop for students who want to learn how to live happier, lower-carbon lives. We start by sharing some of the key food facts we just shared with you. Then, in small groups, the students work together to select changes they want to make in their own lives to cut carbon and get happier. (If you'd like to run a workshop like this for your own students, community group, family, or friends, you can access all our workshop materials for free at happyclimate.org.)

During one of these workshops, a student named Antoine told us that he was planning to give up cheese, now that he recognized its surprisingly high carbon impact. While telling us this, his face crumpled with sadness, as he envisioned his cheeseless future. Being a happiness researcher, Liz could not condone this plan.

Fortunately, cutting back on carbon doesn't have to mean permanently abandoning cheese, corned beef, and other carbon-intensive foods. Just having these high-carbon foods a little less often can make a substantial difference. For example, eating beef once a week, rather than every day, would cut your carbon emissions by more than three tons this year.

And there's more good news: Having high-carbon foods less often might actually enhance your capacity to enjoy them. Liz explored this idea in a study involving chocolate. Although chocolate is a plant-based product, it carries a surprisingly high carbon impact because most chocolate-growing operations entail massive deforestation.[17] In fact, a 3.5 ounce (100 grams) bar of dark chocolate is similar to a lamb chop in terms of carbon emissions (the higher the cacao content, the higher the carbon).

To investigate whether reducing chocolate consumption could enhance the pleasure of eating it, Liz teamed up with Jordi Quoidbach, a psychologist from Belgium who was visiting her lab. True to his Belgian heritage, Jordi loves chocolate—and he's a master of maximizing pleasure. So, he conducted a little experiment, inviting students to come to Liz's lab and taste some chocolate. He measured how much they savored the chocolate—not only by asking them but also by instructing a research assistant to surreptitiously observe how much enjoyment they displayed. Then he gave some of the students, chosen at random, a big bag of chocolate bars. He told them to eat as many as they comfortably could over the next seven days. Meanwhile, he politely asked another group of students to refrain from eating any chocolate for one week. The remaining students were assigned to the control group and didn't receive any special chocolate-related instructions. He brought everyone back to the lab one week later. At their second visit, the students ate some more chocolate and completed measures of savoring, just like in the previous visit.

The first thing that popped out of the data was that the students savored the experience of eating chocolate in the lab less the second week than they had the first week. This simple finding captures what is perhaps the most depressing discovery to emerge from happiness research: The more we repeat a positive experience, the less we tend to appreciate it. Psychologists refer to this process as *hedonic adaptation*.[18] And it has been observed in all kinds of places, with all kinds of people, across a vast range of positive experiences, from receiving money to getting married. For example, one large study found that adults in Germany exhibited a significant increase in happiness when they got married—but then adapted completely, returning to their baseline level of happiness about two years after their wedding day.[19] If you were glowing with happiness when you walked down the aisle, but not when you walked down the stairs to see your spouse at the breakfast table this morning, hedonic adaptation is to blame.

When it comes to food, though, there is a way to short-circuit hedonic adaptation. Jordi discovered that people who had been asked to forgo chocolate for one week exhibited a preserved capacity to savor it. And at the end of the week, they got a bigger happiness boost from eating chocolate compared with the students who had received the bag of candy or had simply continued with their regular consumption habits.[20] So, eating high-carbon foods less often may increase our capacity to enjoy them.

Embracing this sweet spot in her own life, our friend Patricia Houlihan figured out how to get more pleasure from less meat. Patricia is an environmental lawyer and a single mother of twin teenagers. Her family sticks to a plant-forward diet at home, but when they go to restaurants, they order whatever they like. The kids often pick steak. Patricia explains, "If you eat meat every day, you don't really appreciate it. But when you go out for a steak every three or four months, it tastes delicious. It becomes a treat. You look forward to it."

And while it's rare to find meat in Patricia's fridge at home, "When we go to other people's houses," she says, "we have no rules. Whatever they serve, we eat. Because—and I say this to my kids—I don't want us to be the pain-in-the-ass guest that comes over and says, 'We don't eat this. We don't eat that.'"

This approach reduces family friction when she and her kids go to visit her cousins in Alberta (which is known as the Texas of the North). Every year, on Christmas morning, the cousins make bacon. It's a family ritual. And Patricia explains that it makes Christmas special for her kids. As far as they're concerned, eating bacon is like staying in a five-star hotel: It's a special treat that's reserved for important occasions. So, when COVID-19 lockdowns kept her family from visiting the cousins at Christmas, what did Patricia do? She made bacon.

While an annual Day of Bacon works well for Patricia's family, the thought of having bacon just once a year sends shivers down our spines. Singer and cultural icon Beyoncé encouraged her followers to take a more moderate approach, joining her in practicing Meatless Mondays.[21] Meanwhile, her husband, Jay-Z (the *other* JZ), committed to eating two vegan meals per day. Beyoncé explained, "We want to challenge you as we challenge ourselves to move towards a more plant-based lifestyle." And they promised that fans who embraced this challenge would get a chance to win free tickets to both of their shows, for life.

Adopting Meatless Mondays could make a considerable difference. In the United States, the average adult eats a pound of meat per day.[22] So, for these folks, just giving up meat for one day each week would save half a ton of carbon per year.

That said, you could eat meat every day for the rest of your life, while still cutting carbon and enhancing pleasure. The key here is to consider portion size. At Ruth's Chris Steak House in Dallas, the first option on the steak menu is a 16-ounce New York strip[23]—a meal that will cost you 100 pounds of carbon (which is equivalent to driving 112 miles). But you could cut your carbon impact in half by choosing the 8-ounce steak from the same cut, which goes by the name "petite filet," subtly implying it's for children or maybe French people.

At first glance, choosing the smaller steak might seem like a sacrifice. But research suggests that people underestimate the pleasure of smaller portions.[24] For example, in one study, French children were offered tasty snacks, such as brownies, that ranged from the manufacturer's rather modest suggested serving size up to a supersize snack that was more than twice as large.[25] Petite filets aside, it turned out that even French children expected to enjoy the larger snacks more. But unless they were very hungry, their *actual enjoyment* was unrelated to the size of their snack.

How could this be? After all, it seems like more bites of a delicious food should add up to greater pleasure. The culprit here is a basic principle of physiology known as *sensory-specific satiety*.[26] According to this principle, the pleasure of eating a specific food peaks with the first bites, and then begins to decline. Early studies documented this principle in monkeys, whose neurons fired less enthusiastically when they were fed more of the same food—but responded with renewed strength when they were given a different food.[27] If you've ever declared that you're full and then moved on to eat dessert with gusto, you've experienced sensory-specific satiety. As well as explaining the "dessert stomach," sensory-specific satiety underpins food writer Michael Pollan's argument that "the banquet is in the first bite."[28]

Because the first bites are the best, a sixteen-ounce steak may deliver no more pleasure than an eight-ounce steak (unless you are exceptionally hungry). In fact, there is some evidence that larger portions might even undermine our enjoyment of food, at least in retrospect, because the less pleasurable final bites drag down overall evaluations of the meal.[29] These findings led French researchers Pierre Chandon and Yann Cornil to surmise that getting people to focus more on the pleasure of eating might actually help them choose smaller portions.

To explore this idea, they conducted a small study at a cafeteria in France.[30] Diners were invited for a prix fixe lunch and were allowed to choose their own portions for each course. In the control condition, diners received a simple menu, which described the main course as beef shepherd's pie with tomato and pesto sauce. Meanwhile, other diners received an "epicurean" menu that provided more sensual descriptions of the same dishes. For them, the shepherd's pie was described as "Beef subtly seasoned with Espelette pepper under a rich velvety potato puree, topped with crisp parmesan cheese crumbs" (this description sounds even more enticing in French). Compared with those who got the basic menu, diners who received the epicurean menu chose smaller portions—and expected to enjoy the meal more. They also spent more time savoring the food, according to observations the researchers made using cameras hidden in the ceiling.

If you want to experiment with this approach at your next dinner party, try describing your dishes using one of these epicurean words, to invoke savoring: *aromatic, braised, bright, briny, cheesy, chunky, citrusy, crumbly, crunchy, crusty, fluffy, foamy, frothy, gooey, luscious, nutty, pan-fried, peachy, peppery, perfumed, piquant, seared, succulent, sultry, tangy, toasty, velvety,* or *vibrant.*

But be warned: The effectiveness of this approach may hinge on the cultural background of your guests. Pierre and Yann have found that French people are much more likely than Americans to happily select smaller portions in response to epicurean labels. Why? They argue that French people are culturally predisposed to view food as a source of pleasure. In contrast, Americans tend to think of food in more utilitarian terms, focusing on nutrition and value for money. One classic study found that Americans tend to associate desserts like chocolate cake and ice cream with the words *fattening* and *guilt*, whereas the French associate those desserts with *delicious* and *celebration*.[31]

Of course, culture isn't everything, and individuals vary a lot on whether they think about food as a central source of pleasure, so Pierre and Yann created an Epicurean eating scale. You can see how you score (and how you compare to us, and to the French and American research participants).

Epicurean (Pleasure–Seeking) Eating Tendency Scale[32]

Instruction: Rate how much you agree with each statement on a scale from 1 (totally disagree) to 7 (totally agree).

1. If I try, I can clearly and easily imagine the taste of many dishes.

2. My friends say that I am a foodie.

3. Cooking is a major form of art, similar to music or painting.

4. I like to discuss the taste of food with my friends.

5. There is a lot of beauty in food.

6. I can easily find the words to describe the taste of many foods.

7. More than other people, I value the look, the smell, the taste, the texture in mouth of foods.

Scoring: Add up your score for each item and divide the total by 7 to find your overall score. For comparison, in one study with more than 800 American and French adults, the average score was 5.07 for Americans and 5.23 for French people.[33] Liz scored 5.7, while JZ topped out the scale at 6.9.

Research on the value of epicurean eating suggests that focusing on carbon emissions might reinforce the tendency to think of food as merely a means to an end. So, rather than pulling out a carbon calculator at lunchtime, simply elevating pleasure as a central goal of eating may help us savor smaller portions.

JZ takes this approach to the extreme. She scores sky-high

on the epicurean eating scale, but consumes only about fifteen hundred calories per day. Liz finds the prospect of eating so little food mildly horrifying. And abundance does have its place: in the fruit and vegetable aisle.

What Does Broccoli Have to Do with Happiness?

We've already seen that fruits and vegetables are almost uniformly low in terms of carbon, so you can eat as much as you want without a considerable carbon cost. And remarkably, in large-scale surveys, people who report eating more fruits and vegetables tend to score higher on measures of happiness.[34] It's easy to think of explanations for this correlation, though. For one thing, wealthier people eat more fruits and vegetables, and they also tend to be happier. But even when researchers carefully control for individual differences in wealth, the relationship between eating produce and being happy still pops out. In fact, this correlation stubbornly sticks around even when scientists control for a cornucopia of other variables, from exercise and drinking habits to smoking and ethnicity.

Still, it's impossible to control for *everything*. And it could be the case that feeling happy leads people to eat more fruits and vegetables, rather than vice versa. So, correlational evidence can only provide clues about what might make people happy, but it can't tell us for sure. We can get one step closer to figuring out this puzzle by looking at longitudinal studies, in which the same people are followed over time. In one of these studies, a nationally representative sample of approximately fifty thousand people in the UK answered questions about their eating habits and their happiness multiple times over a period of seven years.[35] As it turned out, when individuals increased their fruit and vegetable consumption, they got happier. Conversely, when individuals stopped eating produce, their happiness declined—and the size of the effect was similar to the effect of being widowed.

Not all improvements in healthy eating were linked to enhanced happiness either. British individuals who consumed whole-grain bread and skim milk were no happier than their counterparts who chose white bread and full-fat milk. So, this study suggests there really is something special about fruits and vegetables.

When we told one of our friends about this study, though, she smirked and said, "Yeah, but you know, it's British people." While this might not seem like the most sophisticated scientific critique, it's true that we should always be cautious about generalizing a finding from one country to the rest of the world. But the same basic effect emerged when other researchers examined longitudinal data from a nationally representative sample of more than ten thousand Australians.[36]

Still, if we really want to know whether eating vegetables *causes* improvements in happiness, we need to get people to change their diet, without making other changes in their lives. Taking this approach, researchers recruited seventy-five overweight adults in Grand Forks, North Dakota, who typically ate almost no vegetables (the researchers specified that fried potatoes didn't count as vegetables). Then, they randomly assigned half of these adults to receive free vegetables for eight weeks, while the remaining folks stuck with their regular diet.[37]

Every week, the researchers scanned all participants' skin for a pigment called carotenoids, which is a marker of vegetable consumption. Sure enough, participants in the free-veggie group showed a visible uptick in carotenoids. Meanwhile, those in the diet-as-usual control group didn't show any improvements in their carotenoid levels. And their self-reported happiness levels remained unchanged. But, by the end of the eight-week period, participants in the veggie group exhibited a significant increase in their overall happiness. The researchers speculated that the vitamins and phytochemicals in vegetables provide anti-inflammatory and antioxidant benefits that enhance not only physical health, but mental health, too.

Because we know that participants started eating more vegetables due to the researchers' instructions—not because they got married or experienced some other life event—we can be pretty confident that this dietary change actually *caused* an increase in happiness. We should be careful about overgeneralizing from one small study, but another team of researchers found similar results in a larger experiment with university students in New Zealand.[38] And this experiment was *preregistered*, meaning that the researchers essentially called their shots ahead of time, stating how they would run the study and how they would analyze the data before collecting it (if you want to know why this matters for science, you can nerd out with us in the next text box).

Tamlin Conner, who led the New Zealand study, told us

that most of her participants didn't change their fruit and vege-table consumption by much—only by about one serving a day, on average. But her work suggests that even eating an apple or orange per day can make a small but detectable difference in psychological well-being. And while the physical health benefits of dietary changes can take months or years to develop, the emotional health benefits emerge much faster. In fact, according to Tamlin, if you begin increasing your daily consumption of fruits and vegetables today, you can expect to reap the psychological benefits within a week.

Beyoncé discovered this for herself when she tried a twenty-two-day vegan diet. After describing how much she had struggled with previous diets, she explained, "Not only did I make it through twenty-two days, I felt so incredible! Now . . . I still eat meat, and it's all about balance, but absolutely I make better choices."[39]

Which types of fruits and vegetables should you choose to reap the biggest benefits in terms of happiness? Here, interpret-ing the research is more like reading tea leaves, but Tamlin rec-ommends raw produce. Cooking, canning, and other forms of processing can reduce the vitamins and minerals that scientists believe enhance well-being. So, it's probably better to dip fresh celery in hummus, rather than throwing it in a stew. But cooked celery is better than no celery! And let's face it, frozen fruits and vegetables are often much cheaper than fresh produce. Luckily, the freezing process doesn't reduce vitamins and minerals at all. Adding frozen strawberries or mangoes to a morning smoothie is a relatively cheap and quick way to cut carbon and enhance happiness.

Psychology's Silent Revolution

Over the past decade, psychology has undergone a revolution—but surprisingly, many fans of psychology have never heard of it. Beginning around 2011, researchers in psychology and other scientific fields confronted a "replication crisis," in which some of the field's most prominent findings turned out to be false.[40] Too often, researchers had relied on small samples and had massaged their data to produce the effects they wanted, or expected. This sounds nefarious, but it usually isn't. There are lots of ways to analyze any one data set, and researchers have to make many decisions about how to slice and dice it along the way. For example, should researchers exclude slackers who are told to eat more veggies but don't follow these instructions perfectly? If researchers try running the analysis with and without the slackers and find that their intervention produces significant effects only when the slackers are removed, it's easy to justify leaving them out. But making lots of these little choices can essentially airbrush the data, so the results look stronger than they really are.

To nip this in the bud, researchers like Tamlin Conner have begun to "preregister" their studies: Before handing out fruits and vegetables to college students, Tamlin's team publicly stated exactly how they would run the experiment and how they would analyze the data—effectively tying their own hands so that they couldn't airbrush their data, even inadvertently.

So, if a study is preregistered, you can have more confidence in the results, which is especially important if you're thinking of making a lifestyle change based on it. And it's also worth paying attention to how many people were included in the study. Very small studies often yield unreliable results. For example, the North Dakota study included a mere seventy-five participants, so we would be pretty skeptical if Tamlin hadn't found similar benefits in a larger, preregistered experiment. It also helps that correlational and longitudinal studies provide converging evidence for the idea that fruit and vegetable consumption is linked to happiness. Science always involves wrestling with uncertainty, and we've done this wrestling for you—behind the scenes—for every claim we make in this book.

Change Is Hard

Maybe you've now resolved to eat more fruits and vegetables, choose chicken over beef, or practice Meatless Mondays. Yay!

But if there's one thing we've learned as experts in behavior change, it's that changing behavior over the long term is hard—really, really hard. And this may be especially true when it comes to eating, partly because we are confronted with so many decisions and temptations in a single day. Indeed, one study found that 84 percent of people who tried a vegan or vegetarian diet ended up abandoning it.[41]

So, we would like to arm you with the best strategies that behavioral science has to offer, to help you put your low-carbon eating plans into action. And because mnemonic devices make complicated ideas easier to remember, we've got one for you: *Maximize EASE*. As we explain in the following section, you'll be more likely to successfully stick with low-carbon food choices if you make them *Easy*, *Attractive*, *Social*, and *Eye-catching*.

Make It Easy

Humans like easy things. In fact, this principle extends to almost all creatures, including slime mold. This simple organism—which looks like dog vomit—crawls through space consuming carbohydrates. When scientists place a blob of slime mold at the entrance of a maze, with some oats at the other end, the slime mold finds the shortest path to the food.[42] In one study, researchers used piles of oats to represent the thirty-six cities surrounding Tokyo, and then set the slime mold loose in oat-Tokyo.[43] In just over a day, the mold found the shortest paths connecting the oat-cities, moving through space in an efficient pattern that mirrored the Tokyo rail network.

If all living things gravitate toward the least effortful options, then expecting ourselves to overcome this core principle of life may be a setup for failure. Before her son, Oliver, was born, Liz imagined herself feeding Oliver snacks and meals filled with fresh vegetables. As it turned out, Oliver didn't particularly care for vegetables. But when he arrived home from school—hungry and in search of a snack—he would eat vegetables if they had been cut up and arrayed in a pleasing pattern, with hummus, on the kitchen table. Like the slime mold, Oliver took the shortest path to food.

Liz resolved to have a plate of fresh, appealing vegetables awaiting Oliver each day after school. Alas, she soon discovered how much she, too, had in common with the slime mold. On busy afternoons overstuffed with meetings and emails, she gave up on cleaning and chopping vegetables, handing Oliver a jar of peanut butter and a spoon after school and ordering takeout for dinner.

After wallowing in her failure to juggle parenthood and a full-time job, she hired a college student to come over for a couple of hours after school. This new family helper swooped in and—for less than the cost of takeout—absolved Liz of her mom guilt, by shopping, chopping, and prepping vegetables and other fresh, healthy ingredients for Oliver's after-school snack and the family dinner.

Since then, meal-kit delivery services have sprung up, making low-carbon cooking quicker and easier. For example, the company HelloFresh enables customers to select vegetarian or pescatarian meals to cook at home, with preportioned ingredients left on their doorsteps. And according to HelloFresh, their meal-delivery system reduces carbon emissions by 25 percent compared with purchasing the same ingredients at the supermarket. Most of the savings comes from buying ingredients from more sustainable sources and reducing food waste by providing only the amount of each ingredient that each customer needs.[44] It's always worth being skeptical of corporate claims, but when we did the math ourselves based on their published report, we found the savings was actually higher—around 32 percent. And this math assumes that customers would buy exactly the same meals if they went to the supermarket. But, while dashing through the crowded store after work, it's tempting to forget about climate change and grab whatever meal would be fast and satisfying. By contrast, it's much easier to stick with a commitment to low-carbon eating when all the ingredients are chopped and waiting for you at the end of a busy day. While services like HelloFresh tend to cost a little more per meal than buying the same ingredients at a grocery store, we appreciate not having to fork over money for a whole jar of saffron just to make one dish of Persian chicken.

Make It Attractive

In first-century Rome, an early foodie named Apicius purportedly said, "We eat first with our eyes."[45] Researchers put this adage to the test in a study delightfully titled "A Field Experiment on the Influence of Fun Bread Roll Shape on Breakfast Consumption."[46] They visited a dozen elementary schools in the Netherlands, toting baskets brimming with white bread rolls or healthier, whole-wheat rolls. Most children selected the white bread. But consumption of the healthier option doubled when researchers offered whole-wheat rolls in appealing shapes like fish and hearts.

Adults aren't so different from kids. In one study, British adults were asked to search for recipes using a website built for the experiment.[47] When they typed in a search term like "burger," they were presented with a variety of recipes, ranging from classic options like cheddar bacon burgers to healthier, lower-carbon options such as pumpkin bean burgers. Each recipe was accompanied by a popularity rating and a photo of the dish from Allrecipes. Unbeknownst to participants, the researchers had manipulated the photos, tweaking subtle visual features like color, brightness, and saturation to make each meal a little more or less attractive. Simply presenting a more colorful photo—without changing any of the ingredients—increased adults' proclivity to choose the recipe. In fact, colorfulness mattered three times as much as the recipe's popularity rating. So, a relatively unpopular option like a pumpkin bean burger could be lifted from online oblivion by a single beautiful photo.

Appearance can even affect taste. In a classic wine-tasting study, researchers added varying amounts of red food coloring to glasses of white wine.[48] Simply changing the color changed how the wine tasted to volunteers. And this effect was driven not by novice drinkers, but by wine experts. While it's always fun to trick snobby sommeliers with a little food coloring, the point is that appearance can shape our expectations about taste, which in turn shape our *experiences*. In fact, other studies have shown that simply adding red food coloring to water makes it taste sweeter than adding green food coloring.[49]

Our takeaway isn't that we should bring food-coloring kits to cocktail parties, but simply that we should accept that appearance matters when it comes to food. This idea even applies to food *waste*. Composting is a highly effective strategy for reducing emissions from food waste—but Liz has struggled to stick with this habit because of the revolting sight and smell of rotting banana peels, half-eaten poached eggs, and chicken bones. So, JZ taught her a simple trick to make composting bags a little less gross: Keep them in the freezer. With everything frozen solid and covered in a frosty glaze, even food waste doesn't look too bad.

And attractiveness is also important to consider when making bigger changes. For example, if you're thinking of switching to a plant-forward diet, it could be worth investing in a vegetarian cookbook filled with vibrant, full-color photos that will entice you to try new recipes. Or follow folks on Instagram and YouTube who post stunningly beautiful images of the kinds of food you aspire to eat.

If you're trying to bring your family and friends with you on your food journey, pay extra attention to making sure the food not only tastes good, but looks good, too. Plus, you can tell them that eating a plant-forward diet might actually change the appearance of their skin. The carotenoids in fruits and vegetables impart a more vibrant color to skin. And one study found that—at least among pale British people—this change in skin coloration increased attractiveness more than visiting a tanning salon.[50]

Make It Social

Although the question of what to put in our mouths feels like a deeply personal one, it is also heavily influenced by the other people around us. Our colleagues tested this idea by tracking the lunch orders placed by people standing in line at a café on our campus.[51] Each day, the café offered a meat wrap, a veggie wrap, and two rotating hot entrées, including a meat option (such as rice with curried chicken) and a vegetarian option (such as rice with curried lentils). Remarkably, 72 percent of diners ordered the exact same dish as the random stranger standing in front of them. When the stranger in front ordered meat, only 27 percent of people ordered a vegetarian option—but 47 percent chose a veggie option after witnessing a veggie order.

It's possible that some people listened to the preceding order and intentionally chose the same dish, but most people said their choice was not influenced by what the stranger in front of them selected. Even for folks who claimed that they hadn't been influenced, however, the researchers found a significant effect of the preceding stranger's choice. So, social influence is more powerful than many of us realize.

If the food selected by a random stranger can double our chances of choosing a veggie option, then our friends may exert an even more potent influence on our eating habits. To examine how friends shape each other's choices, researchers at a university in Switzerland analyzed more than sixteen thousand food purchases made by staff and students.[52] Because the staff and students used ID cards to make their purchases, the researchers were able to identify pairs of friends who began regularly eating together. Over a two-year period, these friends mimicked each other's choices. For example, people were more likely to buy fruit if their friend bought fruit.

To harness the power of social influence, you might consider meeting up for meals with friends who have already embraced the eating habits you're striving to adopt. Or, you could form a Low-Carbon Lunch group of colleagues who also care about climate change, and try out plant-rich meals together. Eating with others is typically more enjoyable than eating alone,[53] so this strategy can also enhance happiness for both you and your colleagues.

On the flip side, it's worth recognizing that your goal of climate-friendly eating may be blocked by people who don't share this desire. If your whole family loves meat, then pushing for vegetarian dinners may create friction. So, it might be easier to integrate new eating habits at lunch, or other meals when those family members aren't around. Alternatively, you could take a page from Patricia's book by keeping your own fridge clear of high-carbon foods—but eating whatever friends and family serve you at their houses. And if you decide to stick to your guns and make climate-friendly choices at every meal, you can rest assured that those around you are being influenced by your positive choices—even if they say they're not!

Make It Eye-catching

If you've ever stared into a full fridge and then walked away, concluding that there's nothing to eat, you've experienced what cognitive psychologists call *visual crowding.*[54] Our brains can get overwhelmed by a packed visual scene.

In one study, participants made hundreds of choices between pairs of snacks presented on a computer screen.[55] The researchers subtly manipulated each snack to fade into the background or "pop," like a Marimekko pillow on a beige couch. People were more likely to select snacks that popped out from the background—and this seemingly trivial factor mattered over and above the perceived tastiness of each snack.

Taking this idea out of the lab, a restaurant in Sweden experimented with placing vegetarian dishes front and center on the menu.[56] On the restaurant's original lunch menu, diners first saw a daily meat dish, such as baked lamb leg with pumpkin salad, goat cheese, and eggplant caviar; followed by a daily fish dish, such as breaded flounder with aioli, lilac bread, and pickles. Finally, the end of the menu featured a vague statement noting, "A vegetarian option is available on request." Then, the restaurant flipped the script, creating a new menu that put a vegetarian dish at the top, such as spice-baked pumpkin with crudités, eggplant caviar, and goat cheese. This was followed by a fish dish, and finally a statement that "an option containing meat is available on request." With the old menu, only 2 percent of diners chose the vegetarian option, but this number skyrocketed to 23 percent within one week of introducing the new menu. And while 57 percent of people ordered meat when it was front and center, only 10 percent asked for it with the new menu.

Modern cognitive psychology backs up the old saying that out of sight is out of mind. Unfortunately, refrigerators weren't designed by cognitive psychologists. Instead, our fridges were designed by well-intentioned engineers, who built crisper drawers to keep fresh produce moist. But tucking fruits and vegetables away in drawers can make them easy to forget—until you go looking for the source of the moldy smell in your fridge.

JZ harnessed her PhD in cognitive psychology to feng shui her fridge. She moved her fresh produce from crisper-drawer exile to the fridge doors so that when she opened her fridge, the first thing she saw were fresh fruits and vegetables. Front of fridge, she reasoned, is front of mind. The crisper drawer became the condiment drawer, where ketchup and other long-lasting products found their forever home. She slid soda cans and a bottle of champagne to the back of the fridge, making space—front and center—for leftovers and other fresh food at risk of going bad. JZ shared her fridge makeover in a TED Talk and quickly became the Marie Kondo of refrigeration, inspiring others to follow her lead (for photos of fridges before and after their makeovers, check out happyclimate.org).

Meanwhile, JZ found a new sense of serenity as she cut back on food waste. In North America, the average person wastes almost one pound of food per day,[57] totaling $655 of wasted money per year. And food waste takes up more space than anything else in US landfills,[58] while emitting methane, which is thirty times more potent than carbon dioxide in heating up the planet.[59] So, taking twenty minutes today to feng shui your fridge can make a real difference—and sharing before and after photos can inspire others to do the same.

Beyond Individuals

If you want to stick with a low-carbon diet, it can help to maximize EASE. The strategies we've provided are intended to empower you to make the choices that feel right to you. But there's a tension here: Providing this type of advice can imply that the burden of change rests on individuals alone. And this couldn't be more wrong. Our choices about food are deeply shaped and constrained by the systems and organizations in which we find ourselves. For example, if you live in a food desert, then filling up on fresh produce may feel almost impossible.

The good news is that systems and organizations are made up of individuals, who can spark broader change in ways they never would have imagined. To see how this might work, we'd like to take you to the ultimate food desert—a hospital—along with a celebrity chef named Ned Bell.

Ned has appeared on television shows like *Iron Chef Canada*, but he describes his job simply as "bringing joy to people through food." After graduating from culinary school and making a name for himself, he became the executive chef at the Four Seasons Hotel in Vancouver, where he turned the hotel into a national leader in sustainable seafood practices. He wrote a cookbook called *Lure*, filled with sustainable seafood recipes, and traveled the world speaking about his passion for oceans and rivers.

And then Ned's world changed overnight. His wife, Kate Colley, was diagnosed with breast cancer. Suddenly, their days were dominated by chemo, radiation, and—finally—surgery. After undergoing major surgery and recovering without food for several days, Kate lay in her hospital bed at Vancouver General Hospital (VGH), relishing the thought of finally eating a real meal. But when the much-anticipated meal arrived, Ned says, "We were kind of baffled." The pile of mush in front of Kate was meant to be macaroni and cheese but was barely identifiable, which was astonishing to Ned. As he put it, "It's pretty hard to mess up macaroni and cheese. But they messed it up." He took to social media to express his shock that food like this was being provided to patients, right when they most needed nourishment and comfort.

Kate's surgeon, Dr. Andrea MacNeill, saw the post and reached out to Ned to ask if he would like to help fix the problem. Andrea describes herself as an "eco-surgeon," and she wanted to overhaul the food offered at VGH, not only to improve patients' experiences but also to reduce carbon emissions. So, the chef and the surgeon teamed up, along with JZ and her PhD student Annie Lalande. They built a new planetary health menu centered on the principles described in this chapter, eliminating beef while elevating plants and sustainable proteins.

But Ned soon encountered challenges at the hospital that he'd never considered at the Four Seasons. For one thing, the hospital budgeted less than ten dollars a day to feed each patient, and this wasn't about to change. And because safety was the paramount concern, all food had to be cooked to at least 160 degrees—which, Ned explains, means "you're never going to eat a beautiful piece of asparagus at a hospital." Plus, the hospital relied almost exclusively on frozen vegetables. Ned quickly discovered that he could flex his culinary skills to make frozen peas and carrots palatable, but, he concluded, "Frozen cauliflower is gross. And a frozen bell pepper? No thank you."

He begged for fresh vegetables, but the hospital couldn't afford the labor required to clean and chop them. So, Ned found companies that provided affordable, prepackaged raw vegetables, already cleaned and chopped. He coated them in his own bright, vibrant sauces and dressings, banning the little plastic packages of Kraft salad dressing that patients expected to see on their trays. To control costs (and carbon), Ned used relatively small portions of the pricier proteins as garnish atop healthy grains and vegetables. The new menu included flavorful, low-carbon dishes like a Thai noodle bowl with tofu and bok choy, and steelhead trout with a maple-lime glaze.

JZ and Annie surveyed hundreds of patients before and after the new menu was introduced,[60] asking them to rate each meal they ate in the hospital. Before the new menu, the typical meal scored in the "okay" range (which, frankly, seemed generous). But afterward the meals were rated as "good." And these new meals generated 50 percent less carbon.

Leaving these numbers aside, what really mattered was that patients said food had become a source of pleasure for them during a terrible time in their lives. After tasting the steelhead trout, one patient said, "I forgot I was in pain for a little while."

And if it's possible to enhance enjoyment and cut carbon in a public hospital, then we are optimistic that this approach can work just about anywhere.

CHAPTER 3

How to Buy Low-Carbon Happiness

If aliens landed on Earth and wanted to understand why humans consume so much carbon, we would start our tour at a seven-year-old's birthday party. At a typical party, throngs of children arrive clutching gifts—often purchased by harried parents the night before—and leave with goodie bags full of trinkets. Most of the gifts and goodies provide fleeting delight before being stuffed into closets. In response to this cycle of overconsumption, it's become fashionable to end a birthday invitation with the words "No gifts, please." This instruction is ignored by most people—except Liz, who showed up empty-handed at one party and was promptly shamed by the hostess.

Kyla Hunter, an optometrist in northern Canada, found a happier way to cut carbon by throwing her daughter Kacela a "Toonie Party." Instead of gifts, each guest was asked to bring a two-dollar coin (fondly known as a toonie in Canada). Half the money went to Kacela so she could treat herself to one special present, and the other half went to charity. Gone was the austerity and ambiguity of "No gifts, please." In its place was a simple instruction that eliminated shopping time for all the guests, leaving Kacela with something she really wanted.

Kyla told us, "I hate the stress of finding a present for a kid in a preschool class I barely even know." In the spirit of inclusivity, she explained, "Everyone gets invited to everybody's birthday. So then you go to this birthday party with twenty kids, and there's this mound of presents." Opening the first few is exciting for the birthday boy or girl. "But by the time they're opening present number fifteen, they're kind of over it." It's like a master class in hedonic adaptation, for preschoolers.

And Kyla added, "It's really expensive for parents. If you're spending twenty dollars per birthday gift and there are twenty kids in the class, then that's a good chunk of money over the year, just for birthday presents that nobody needs."

By receiving toonies instead, Kacela not only got to buy herself a gift, but she also got to choose how to use half of her birthday money to help someone else. Kyla and Kacela spent time scrolling through the website of a charity called Plan International, which enables donors to fund specific gifts to help disadvantaged children, from food baskets and books to school supplies and medicine. Kacela decided to use her birthday toonies to fund a newborn health checkup. "I would talk excitedly about the toonie party and ask her who she was going to share her money with," Kyla explained. "The response was always, 'The tiny little baby!' Kacela would ask me to pull up the picture on my computer so that she could see the baby."

Kyla wrote about this experience on her blog, and it was shared all over the internet and picked up by radio stations.[1] The story reached Liz, who decided to throw a toonie party for her son, Oliver. Oliver wasn't so into newborn babies, but he loved puppies, so he gave his birthday money to the local animal shelter. Liz took Oliver to donate his toonies at the shelter, where he got to meet the animals he was helping—an experience that stuck with him long after the special present he had chosen for himself was forgotten.

The toonie party is contagious because it effectively reduces overconsumption and hedonic adaptation, while saving time and promoting the joy of giving. Children's birthday parties are just the beginning. Everyday life affords numerous opportunities to spend, save, and invest money in ways that enhance happiness and cut carbon.

Shopping Misconceptions

If you try to picture a climate-conscious shopper, you might envision someone strolling through a farmers market, sipping water from a stainless steel bottle and toting an organic cotton bag filled with local produce. But this shopper's good intentions may have hidden carbon costs.

According to a report from Denmark's Ministry of Environment, an organic cotton bag needs to be used more than

150 times—and a regular cotton bag, more than fifty times—to offset its carbon costs relative to a single-use plastic bag.[2] Growing cotton organically isn't easy, resulting in low yields that jack up carbon costs.[3] Other crops lend themselves better to organic methods, but with the exception of fruit, buying organic doesn't reduce carbon costs and can even increase them.[4]

If we look beyond carbon and consider water use, land use, pollution, and other environmental costs, then a regular cotton bag needs to be used more than seven thousand times. And an organic cotton bag must be used a whopping twenty thousand times—in other words, you would need to use the bag twice a week for two hundred years just to break even with plastic bags.

We don't mean to sound pro-plastic; after all, it's reasonable to be haunted by images of discarded plastic floating in the ocean and to worry about the potential health problems with microplastics. Surprisingly, though, when it comes to microplastics, new research suggests that plastic straws and cups may actually be less harmful than paper straws[5] and cups[6] (because of the plastic coating applied to these paper alternatives). As for that stainless steel bottle, you need to use it about fifty times to offset its carbon impact relative to a single-use plastic bottle.[7] These statistics complicate our assumptions about sustainable shopping.

So, what's an environmentally conscious shopper to do? It's sensible to buy a small number of reusable bags and mugs, with the goal of using each one as many times as possible. To make this happen, consider storing them in your car or wherever you will need them. Too often, Liz has found herself on an unplanned grocery run, which inevitably results in her feeling guilty about asking for a plastic bag. So, she forks over the money for yet another "reusable" bag, later stuffing it into her closet at home. In this case, ditching the guilt and asking for a plastic bag would be the more climate-friendly option.

Climate guilt can also lead us to make counterproductive choices about how and where to shop. Many people assume it's better for the climate to buy local than to shop online. But while there are many good reasons to shop locally, such as a desire to support small-business owners, this approach doesn't have much of an impact on climate change—and it can even be counterproductive. In fact, compared with driving store-to-store, online shopping can cut emissions in half.[8] Delivery services typically use more efficient vehicles than ordinary consumers do, and they plan highly efficient routes—not necessarily because they care about climate change, but because this approach is essential to their bottom line. And shopping ranks among the least happy activities in a typical day.[9] So, if online shopping saves you from spending precious minutes of your day sitting in traffic, searching for parking, and waiting in line, then it's likely to be a good investment in your happiness, too.

That said, online shopping does have one major pitfall: excessive returns. Because many sites offer free returns, it's tempting to order five new pairs of jeans in various sizes and styles, try them on in the comfort of your home, then keep the best pair and return the other four. The problem is the four rejects are then at high risk of ending up in a landfill. Online shopping works best when you know exactly what you want.

All else being equal, what you buy matters more than where it comes from. For example, eating edamame shipped from South America has a much lower carbon cost than eating beef raised on a local farm. Of course, flying Maine lobsters to California for a dinner party is another story. But if food and other products are shipped by sea, then the carbon costs are surprisingly trivial.[10] IKEA estimates that just 5 percent of the company's climate impact stems from transporting products, and a mere 1 percent from product delivery; the lion's share comes from the materials themselves.[11]

So, if a big chain store or online retailer uses sustainable materials, buying what you need from them can be more effective for cutting carbon than shopping at a locally owned store in your neighborhood. But it isn't always easy to identify which brands are genuinely committed to minimizing carbon. According to a 2024 global survey, 80 percent of consumers were willing to pay more for sustainable products, which makes it tempting for companies to portray their products as carbon-light, even if they're not.[12] One study found that simply placing a car against a natural background filled with greenery led consumers to perceive the car as more eco-friendly.[13] To spot this kind of greenwashing, watch out for vague labels like "all-natural," "green," and "eco-friendly," not to mention totally irrelevant labels like "non-GMO." Instead, look for transparent and specific carbon reporting (like the IKEA stats we cited in the preceding paragraph).

Maybe this all sounds completely overwhelming. But while some common shopping recommendations turn out to be problematic, there are things each of us can do that have a big impact—and they can make us happier, too. In the pages that follow, we offer several simple principles for cutting carbon and getting more joy from your money.

Buy Nicer Things

Angel Chang did not grow up in a hotbed of high fashion. She was raised in Muncie, Indiana, a town where, she told us, "Fashion didn't exist." As a teenager, she announced that she wanted to be a fashion designer, and her parents were appalled. "My mom thought I wanted to be a seamstress," Angel said. So, Angel wrote a letter to her favorite designer, Anna Sui. Remarkably, Anna wrote back. She told Angel that her parents hadn't wanted her to become a fashion designer either, and she encouraged Angel to move to New York City to get an education and an internship in fashion. Angel took this advice to heart, attending Barnard College in Manhattan. "Two weeks before school started, I went to Anna Sui's store in Soho, and she happened to be there," Angel said. "She remembered the letter, and she offered me an internship."

After graduating, Angel got a job as a designer with Donna Karan. She wrote runway reviews for *Vogue France* and was featured as one of the fashion world's top new talents in the "Beautiful People" issue of *Paper* magazine. It was the stuff of dreams. But these experiences also gave her a window into the darker side of the fashion industry. Angel was inspired to start her own line of high-fashion sustainable clothing, Angel Chang womenswear, which embraced traditional, Indigenous craftsmanship.

Over coffee, Angel told us how the industry works to create "artificial fashion trends." These trends used to be centered on the four seasons, "so, people would just buy spring, summer, fall, and winter." But fast-fashion brands like Zara changed the cadence to every two weeks. "They're pumping all these clothes out, and then they do all this digital marketing, where they're suddenly telling people, 'Okay, everyone should wear purple.' And it suddenly makes you have that desire."

In a typical year, the fashion industry generates twice the global emissions of all flights and shipping combined (and for that reason, we focus heavily on fashion in this chapter).[14] If you've ever felt the urge to buy and discard clothing with each new season, you've felt the influence of fast fashion. But hedonic adaptation applies here, too. When we're constantly buying new things, we tend to enjoy each purchase a little less. So, buying fewer, nicer things can potentially enhance our pleasure while reducing carbon. To do this, we should start by understanding where the biggest carbon-cutting opportunities lie.

Some types of clothing generate heftier emissions than others. Jeans top the list at seventy-three pounds of carbon a pop,[15] more than the carbon cost of an iPhone 16. In contrast, the average shirt generates only fourteen pounds.[16] This means it's not so bad to buy a trendy T-shirt, but it's wise to invest in just a few high-quality pairs of jeans that can be worn for years. The lowest emissions of all come from underwear; thirty pairs produce lower emissions than a single pair of jeans.[17]

JZ took this information to heart and invested in a thirty-day supply of underwear, which enables her to do laundry just once a month. This might seem a little extreme, but doing less laundry represents a true sweet spot—an opportunity to cut carbon and enhance happiness in one fell swoop. When approximately eight thousand adults in the UK were asked to keep diaries of their daily activities and rate their enjoyment of each one, laundry ranked near the bottom—even below shopping.[18] And washing clothes less frequently helps them last longer. So, we invite you to join JZ in a thirty-day No Laundry Challenge—you'll save time and carbon.

Another satisfying way to fight back against fast fashion is to build a small, beautiful collection of clothing that is made to last. Angel discovered this strategy as an exchange student in Paris. She and her fellow Americans arrived with giant suitcases, and when they saw the tiny closets that awaited them, they couldn't figure out where to put all their clothes. She watched how the fashionable French students would wear one outfit for a whole week. "But, you never know it's the same clothing because they accessorize it. And they look super chic."

She gave us a crash course in this approach to crafting a capsule wardrobe. First, pick your base color: black, brown, or blue. If your whole wardrobe is organized around a single color, then it's easy to swap out items and create varied looks from a small closet. Angel recommends starting with a pair of shoes and working your way up. A nice pair of jeans might come next. High-quality shoes and jeans can be expensive, but instead of focusing on the price tag, consider the cost per wear. If you buy a cheap pair of jeans from a fast-fashion brand and wear them all the time, they'll fall apart quickly. So, treating yourself to a higher-quality pair may be less costly in the long run—and will certainly lower your carbon costs.

Of course, more expensive clothes don't always last longer. If you want to build a high-quality, sustainable wardrobe, it's worth looking for brands that stand behind their clothing by including repairs in the purchase cost. For example, the UK brand Fanfare offers a lifetime promise on all its clothing, providing repairs on their products through a partnership with the aptly named company Clothes Doctor. And the Dutch brand O My Bag not only offers mail-in repairs but will also reimburse customers for hiring a local artisan to repair their bag.

As a fashion designer, looking good is almost part of Angel's job description, but, she says, "I hate shopping." So, she keeps her outfits simple. "I just wear the same thing every day: knee-high leather boots, a shirtdress, and a cashmere sweater." This outfit clashes with our stereotypical image of a climate-conscious, tree-hugging hippie. But by wearing these items over and over, Angel keeps the costs under control, while looking fabulous.

Going beyond clothing, it's crucial to consider when investing in nicer things matters. To figure out how to spend money in ways that meaningfully impact our happiness, Chris Hsee, a professor at the University of Chicago, identified two types of variables: Type A and Type B.[19]

Type A variables are things that we have an innate, stable, and widely shared ability to assess; Chris offers examples such as "ambient temperature, amount of sleep, concentration of porridge, and the presence or absence of orgasm." While orgasms and porridge don't seem to have much in common—and are rarely mentioned in the same sentence—they both help to satisfy our basic physical needs. In contrast, he argues that we lack any innate capacity to assess the value of Type B variables, such as "the weight of a diamond, the brand of a purse, or the horsepower of a car." Of course, we can quickly *learn* to evaluate Type B variables and take pleasure in a six-carat diamond ring, a Birkin bag, or a Dodge Durango SRT Hellcat. But our enjoyment of these products hinges on comparing ourselves to others, which means that my happiness depends on someone else having less.

To test these ideas, Chris surveyed nearly seven thousand people in thirty-one cities across China. He asked them how happy they felt when they thought about their jewelry (a Type B variable), and then he asked them to report its total value. People felt happier with their own jewelry if it was more valuable compared with the jewelry collections of others in the same city, suggesting that jewelry might be a good investment in happiness. But when Chris looked *across* cities, the relationship between jewelry value and happiness evaporated. In wealthier cities like Shanghai and Beijing, people owned more jewelry, on average, than in poorer cities like Wuhan. But living in a jewelry-rich city didn't seem to confer any benefit; all that mattered was having more valuable jewels than others in the same city. In other words, the emotional benefits of bling appear to hinge on comparing ourselves favorably with those in our immediate surroundings.

Then, Chris turned his attention to temperature, a Type A variable. During the winter, he asked people how happy they felt when they thought about their current room temperature. These temperatures ranged from an average of sixty-nine degrees in some cities to a frigid fifty-seven in others. JZ grew up in Hangzhou, one of the chillier cities, where central heating was virtually nonexistent. She remembers huddling by the one oil heater in her home and seeing her breath as she tried to stay warm. Sure enough, Chris's data showed that people in Hangzhou felt happier when they were in warmer rooms. But unlike with jewelry, this pattern held up across the country: When it came to room temperature, happiness was tied to physical comfort, not to having a warmer room than one's neighbors. This suggests that improving heating systems can enhance happiness in an absolute sense, apart from the effects of social comparison.

Ironically, however, the climate movement traces its roots to a speech in which President Jimmy Carter encouraged people to do just the opposite, by turning down their thermostats. Sitting in a cardigan sweater by a roaring fire, Carter told Americans, "All of us must learn to waste less energy. Simply by keeping our thermostats, for instance, at 65 degrees in the daytime and 55 degrees at night, we could save half the current shortage of natural gas."[20]

Kevin McCarthy told *The Washington Post* that he remembers the speech vividly. "I was in the sixth grade, I turned on the TV, and I watched Jimmy Carter have a sweater on and tell me to turn the heating down," McCarthy said. "He told me that the best days were behind us, that as an American I had to accept less."[21] McCarthy was inspired to become a Republican and later served as Speaker of the House. Even Jimmy Carter's own vice president, Walter Mondale, expressed some reservations about the degree of self-sacrifice that Carter's approach entailed. "He turned off the air conditioners, and it was so hot in the White House," Mondale recalled. "It would be a hundred above in there."

Fortunately, things have changed. Consumers today don't face such a stark trade-off between enjoying creature comforts and saving on oil and gas. Since Carter's sweater speech, the cost of carbon-free solar energy has come down by multiple orders of magnitude. And heat pumps now enable people to cool their homes in the summer and warm them in the winter, while using very little energy. In fact, compared with turning down the heat and bundling up in a sweater, installing a heat pump would save ten times as much carbon—and installing solar would save twenty times as much.

Of course, in most areas of the world, buying solar panels or heat pumps still entails a considerable outlay of cash. But Chris's research—and JZ's childhood memories—suggests that these may be exceptionally good investments in low-carbon happiness.

Beyond solar panels and heat pumps, a key sweet spot lies in investing more in Type A purchases and less in Type B purchases. Most material things are closer to Type B; our enjoyment depends at least in part on knowing we have bigger diamonds, faster cars, or more stylish handbags than other people. But some purchases don't require any social comparison at all to enjoy: a perfectly ripe mango, a pair of rain boots that are truly waterproof, or a comfortable bed that helps us sleep through the night. By spending our hard-earned money on Type A purchases and forgoing Type B purchases, we can enhance our happiness, cut carbon, and help others resist the siren song of social comparison, too.

Reusing Beats Recycling

A mantra of the environmental movement is "Reduce, Reuse, Recycle." And when JZ and her colleagues asked more than five hundred people in North America to identify the single most effective action they could take to cut carbon, recycling ranked near the very top.[22] But in reality, recycling makes almost no difference.[23] The process of recycling itself requires a lot of energy. Ironically, people's good intentions can make things worse: When overzealous recyclers try to dispose of a greasy pizza box, they can contaminate the whole recycling bin (a tendency known as "wishcycling").

In contrast, reusing existing products can make a substantial difference—but almost no one mentioned this powerful strategy in JZ's study. For Pete Moe, the benefits of reuse became clear after he moved from New York City to Orcas Island in the Pacific Northwest. "I worked in marketing and advertising, but I wasn't very happy," he told us, reflecting on his former life. "I was basically selling garbage to the world." Moving to Orcas changed his relationship with garbage. "When you live on an island, you're surrounded by a moat of water. So, you feel weird when you throw something away and you know it's going to go on a boat to a landfill four hundred miles away."

Pete repurposed his professional skills and became executive director of a nonprofit organization on the island that not only provides recycling but also operates a reuse store called the Exchange. "There's a lot of very wealthy people here now—more so since the pandemic—which has made it harder for working-class people to even afford to live here." Economic inequality is consistently linked to lower levels of happiness,[24] but on Orcas Island, the wealthier residents bring in quality housewares and clothing, which are resold for just a few dollars to people who need them. "It's a huge benefit to the full-time working-class community here. And it makes the wealthier people feel good."

The Exchange has also become a community hub for the island. Many people drop off their recycling and garbage once a week, and they'll pop into the shop next door to donate a few items others might want or to see what's available. "People meet there and hang out and socialize," Pete said. "You see your neighbors." These social interactions might seem trivial, but Liz's research has shown that they can make a measurable difference. On days when people have more interactions with neighbors and other "weak ties," they tend to feel a greater sense of belonging and happiness.[25]

In the years since Pete left New York, buying secondhand has taken on a new sheen in big cities, especially when it comes to clothing. Eco-conscious young people have sought out thrifting as an escape from fast fashion. On TikTok, Macy Eleni (@MacyEleni) posts popular videos like "Thriftmas Eve" and

"The Ultimate Thrift Store Scavenger Hunt," documenting her thrilling finds at estate sales, flea markets, and thrift stores. Her mantra is "Everything hot already exists." And she takes pride in her discoveries. As she puts it, "Thrifting is a goddamn superpower."

Macy lives in Los Angeles—a mecca of thrift stores—but online consignment and thrift stores like ThredUp, the RealReal, and Poshmark have made this approach to shopping accessible to those outside big cities. ThredUp's mission is to "inspire a new generation to think secondhand first." People who want to resell their clothes can simply stuff them into a postage-paid bag, and ThredUp does the rest, checking that the items are in good shape, posting them online, and then sending the seller cash after the items sell. On a typical day, the site has more than four million items of clothing on sale, with brands ranging from Gap to Gucci. We like ThredUp because they provide transparent reporting on their carbon emissions. And according to their calculations, by enabling people to buy used instead of new, ThredUp has saved their customers approximately 800 million pounds of carbon—and more than $6 billion. Right below the sale price for each item, ThredUp displays the estimated retail price to buy the item new, letting customers see just how much money they're saving by buying used. This knowledge may help reduce what economists call the "pain of paying," the twinge of discomfort we feel when we fork over our hard-earned money for the things we desire. Because the pain of paying can drag down the pleasure of consumption, knowing that we're getting a good deal can make buying secondhand more enjoyable than buying new.

Of course, the best way to eliminate the pain of paying is to pay nothing at all. And this strategy is increasingly feasible thanks to an idea dreamed up just south of Orcas Island, in the Puget Sound. On Bainbridge Island, Rebecca Rockefeller and Liesl Clark started the Buy Nothing Project, with the mission "to build resilient communities where our true wealth is the connections forged between neighbors." The Buy Nothing Project now has its own app, but it started as a simple Facebook campaign. One of our own neighbors, Mary Bennett, learned about this project in 2019. She was among the first members of a Buy Nothing group in Kitsilano, the seaside Vancouver neighborhood where Liz and Mary both live. The premise was simple: People could post anything they wanted to give away for free or ask for anything they needed. And they could share words of gratitude with the community. No money would be involved, and even trades were forbidden.

The group grew so fast that it began to spin off smaller groups, including a hyperlocal Buy Nothing group led by Mary. "My group is now just five blocks by five blocks," Mary said, but it includes 850 members. "People join because they want free stuff, or they're moving or downsizing. But what they get is a sense of community and a place to practice generosity and gratitude."

"Halloween often starts in early September," Mary told us. Pumpkin costumes are passed down to neighborhood toddlers. And there are lots of specific requests, too. Someone might post, "'My teenage daughter wants to be this anime character, and I need a blue sash and pink socks.' They could go to the dollar store and buy those things, but that's not good for the environment, and it's a waste of money," Mary said. "And somebody in the neighborhood probably has some pink socks in their bottom drawer that they haven't worn in a year."

Mary remembers one woman posting that she was in the middle of baking and had suddenly realized that she needed a tablespoon of molasses. Rather than buying a whole bottle at the store, she posted to the group. And sure enough, a neighbor showed up on her doorstep with a tablespoon of molasses.

These small gifts among neighbors create a warm feeling of community. One parent in the group told Mary, "We walk around the neighborhood with our kid saying, 'See, that's Mary's house. Remember when we got some soup from her? Oh, there's Carolyn and her dog. Remember we gave them the dog treats our dog didn't like?'"

Sometimes people want to sell their stuff or ask for something in return, but Mary gently reminds them that everything needs to be offered for free, with no strings attached. "I mean, if it was a friend of mine, and I had something I didn't need anymore, I wouldn't say, 'Hey, Kiley, I think this jacket that doesn't fit me might work for you. Would you like it for three dollars?'"

Indeed, research shows that free is a very special price, changing the way people feel and behave.[26] When money is involved, people follow market norms—but when something is free, they attend to social norms instead. In one small study, some students were offered Starburst for a penny each, and they bought an average of about four candies. When other students were told the candy was free, most of them accepted the treat, but they showed more restraint, helping themselves to just one piece.

In another study, some participants were offered Hershey's chocolate for free or for a penny, while others were offered higher-quality Lindt chocolate for either twelve or thirteen cents.[27] Then they were presented with a series of smiley faces, ranging from unhappy to very happy, and they were asked to circle the one that matched their feelings about the offer. While the authors argue that "a Lindt at 13 cents provides a much better deal than a Hershey's at any price," the free chocolate was the runaway winner, yielding by far the biggest smiles.

Mary sees these smiles as she walks around her neighborhood. As an admin of the Buy Nothing group, she's become a kind of neighborhood celebrity. People will say, "'Oh, hi, Mary!' And I know they must be a Buy Nothing friend." When Mary had a hip replacement, one of those Buy Nothing friends delivered her library books for six months.

For Darya Ivanova, an Eastern European immigrant and single mother of two young girls, the Buy Nothing groups in Kitsilano have been life-changing. "I come from a culture where it's not appropriate to share used clothes or other used items. It's considered shameful not to be able to afford something new for your children." It took her many years to change her attitude, and now she's proud to be raising her children with a very different mindset. She gets clothes for her daughters through the Buy Nothing groups, and her kids "love it because it gives them a sense of belonging. It gives them a feeling that somebody else cares for them, and I always tell them, 'This comes from another child who doesn't need it anymore, but they want to share it with you.'" And when her kids outgrow something, Darya said, "If it's still usable, they help clean it, pack it up, and give it to someone else. People send pictures of themselves using these items, which the kids really appreciate because they love that somebody else is enjoying their favorite toy or dress now."

At Christmastime, the girls pack up their old toys into a box and leave it under the tree. "They know that Santa comes and takes the toys and gives them to somebody else, and he brings gifts from somebody else to them." Because she doesn't have to spend a lot of money to provide nice things for her children, Darya has been able to reduce her work hours. Now she works part-time as a paralegal, and she says, "I have time to spend with my children. I have time to cook." And if someone needs a little molasses, she has time to bring it to them.

Neighborhoods aren't the only places where circular gift economies can create feelings of joy and community. Liz teaches a large undergraduate class in social psychology, and throughout the semester, she gives her students a chance to complete a series of optional challenges. When grades are on the line, students get a hungry, mean look in their eyes, so instead of giving them grades for these challenges, Liz gives them "psych gold." At the end of the semester, they can spend their gold in an auction. Liz seeds the auction with several prizes, including free meals and donations to charities selected by the winning students. But the real magic comes from the students themselves, many of whom donate prizes to the auction. Liz invokes Marie Kondo and tells them to look around their homes and find anything that no longer sparks joy for them. Homemade gifts are welcome, too.

In a recent auction, one student contributed a loaf of sourdough bread she had made that morning, while others brought in board games, scented candles, and scarves. One student contributed gold Magnum condoms (in their original packaging). Every single unwanted possession found a new owner. And during a point in the semester when students look weary and downtrodden, the classroom was filled with laughter and cheering, as delighted students claimed their treasures.

Saving and Investing Money

When it comes to cutting carbon, where you stash your money may matter even more than how you spend it. If you have a thousand dollars sitting in a savings account at a major US bank, your money is probably generating about as much carbon each year as if you sent it on a one-way flight from New York to Seattle. In a stunning report, the nonprofit organization Project Drawdown examined data for eleven of the largest US banks, such as Wells Fargo, Bank of America, JPMorganChase, and Capital One.[28] The report revealed that in 2022, these major banks gave around 20 percent of their loans to fossil-fuel companies and other industries that are most responsible for the climate crisis. So, you might be unwittingly loaning 20 percent of your personal savings to these companies.

Luckily, there are good alternatives. To find banks and credit unions that won't use your money to exacerbate the climate crisis, check out the nonprofit organization As You Sow, which offers a database of banks and credit unions that won't use your money to exacerbate the climate crisis. Thanks to the advent of online banking, you have the freedom to choose one that aligns with your values. For the typical American, switching to a climate-friendly bank would make more of a difference than switching to a vegan diet.

If you're not sure where your bank stands on climate, you could simply google "Does [name of your bank] invest in fossil fuels?" When Liz googled this for her credit union, Vancity, the first link contained a clear and unambiguous statement: "We do not invest capital or assets in oil, gas or coal companies." If your financial institution has the answer you want to see, it's not complicated. You can also call or email them and pose the same simple question (for a prewritten email, go to happyclimate.org). If your bank dodges the question by telling you about "sustainability initiatives" like paperless statements, you have your answer. As the writer Neil Simpson put it in a delightful blog, a bank might say, "'We are sustainable because we recycle all of our waste and use solar energy to power our offices.' If that bank is also helping others to extract fossil fuels however, it might as well put its solar panels in a cave on the moon."[29]

Of course, switching banks doesn't sound like the *most* fun thing you could do on a Saturday. But while many pro-climate actions require sustained effort, switching banks is something you can do once and then reap the carbon savings for years. So, if you love steak and international travel, then devoting one afternoon to moving your money might make you happier than changing your diet or your flights.

If you have a 401(k) or other investment account, you have an even bigger opportunity to cut carbon. As many as 99 percent of 401(k) holders are invested in fossil fuels, though many of them don't realize it.[30] Alex Wright-Gladstein confronted this problem as a cofounder and CEO of a climate-tech company called Ayar Labs. "We started offering a retirement plan to our employees, and I asked for a climate-friendly investment option in the lineup," she told us. It took more than three years to get one. "So, for over three years at a climate-tech company, we were requiring all our employees to invest in Exxon and Chevron. And I was like, 'Why is this so hard?'"

As it turns out, it's so hard in part because companies can get sued if they offer their employees 401(k) funds that have unusually high fees or weak performance, so companies are apprehensive about trying anything new in this space. And to be fair to these companies, money does matter for happiness. In fact, while classic research pointed to the conclusion that the emotional benefits of money level off completely once people attain a basic level of comfort, newer research suggests that there is no point at which the emotional benefits of money completely plateau.[31]

If knocking oil and gas out of your portfolio meant accepting lower retirement savings, then taking the moral high ground might leave you less happy. But when Alex dug into the data, she discovered that oil and gas had the worst returns of any economic sector in the past decade. In fact, if you invested $10,000 in oil and gas back in 2014, then ten years later, you would have just $10,004. "It's like investing in the horse-and-buggy industry a century ago," Alex told us. "For people saving for retirement, it just doesn't make sense. It's an industry in decline."

So, Alex founded a new company called Sphere, which offers a low-cost index fund for 401(k)s that tracks the five hundred largest US companies, minus the fossil fuel ones. And Sphere makes an impact by using their clients' shares to push for change at the companies in their portfolio.

But even people who don't invest with Sphere can use their own shares to shape companies' decisions. "Most people don't realize that as shareholders, they have the right to vote at every shareholder meeting at every company they're invested in," Alex said. In other words, while many individuals wish that big companies like Amazon and Walmart would adopt more pro-climate policies, they don't know that—as *owners* of the companies—they can vote on the companies' policies.

Indeed, this was news to Liz. Alex explained that, like Liz, most regular investors don't know their own power. "They aren't offered the opportunity to vote, and honestly, most people don't have the time to even think about it." Rather than individuals voting their own shares, the fund managers end up voting on their behalf. "And those big asset-management firms that are offered in 401(k)s are voting against ninety-eight percent of shareholder proposals having to do with climate change," Alex told us. Most fund managers prioritize profit above all else. So, even though most Americans care about climate change, their shares are being used to vote against pro-climate policies at the biggest companies.

Jason Jay, who directs the MIT Sloan Sustainability Initiative, calls this paradox "zombie capitalism" because almost no one is voting the shares they rightfully own, thereby ushering in a future that no one wants. And he's building a movement to fix it, by making it easy for ordinary investors to delegate their shares—not to big fund managers, but to nonprofit organizations, such as those that are focused on fighting climate change (you can learn more about the movement at www.Shareholder Democracy.org). This means anyone who owns stock can regain control of their power—without having to spend a miserable Saturday reading shareholder proposals for the hundreds of companies included in the fund.

In fact, Andy Behar, leader of As You Sow, made it his mission to keep this process from sucking up ordinary investors' precious time. "We interviewed a lot of people, and we said, 'Look, if it's one click to create a livable planet for you and your pets and your children, would you do it?' And they're like, 'Yeah.' And so we said, 'Well, what about two clicks?' And they're like, 'I don't know. I've got cat videos to watch. I'm busy.'"

Rather than throwing up his hands in exasperation, Andy and his team worked hard to get the whole process down to one click. "We've created a platform called As You Vote," he said. "And with one click, you're voting every item on every ballot, and it's free." Andy estimates that in the United States, 100 million people own $7 trillion in stock that they could be using to assert power, if only they took advantage of shareholder voting rights.

"Money is power. But most people abdicate their power by handing it off to some financial adviser," Andy told us. And these advisers tend to invest in the status quo. "Taking back your power should give you some sense of joy," he said. "Because right now we feel so disassociated from our own power."

And reasserting shareholder power can make a remarkable difference. Just ask Costco. Their emissions exceed those of the entire country of Argentina.[32] So, a tiny organization called Green Century Funds submitted a shareholder proposal asking Costco to set ambitious carbon-reduction targets. Then, they got a broad swath of investors on board. As a result, in 2022, the giant wholesaler was effectively forced by shareholders to reduce emissions across their entire global supply chain.[33]

Costco could be just the beginning. Andy estimates that individual investors own around 20 percent of just about every major company. He often hears from people who complain that the big three investment firms—BlackRock, State Street, and Vanguard—have all the money, and all the power. "And I say, no, BlackRock has no money at all. BlackRock has *our* money—and our permission to use it against us. As does Vanguard, as does State Street." But now you can take back that permission, with just a click, by signing up for As You Vote, or investing with a pro-climate fund like Green Century or Sphere.

Donating Money

A few years ago, Liz got one of the most amazing phone calls of her life. It was Chris Anderson, the head of TED. Liz and Chris had gotten to know each other back in 2019, when Liz gave a TED Talk on her research showing that generosity promotes happiness. In one of her earliest experiments on this topic, her research assistants approached people on campus and handed them either a five-dollar or twenty-dollar bill. Some of them were asked to spend this money to benefit others—and they wound up feeling happier by the end of the day than those assigned to spend the money on themselves. This early finding made headlines around the world because it highlights a beautiful aspect of human nature: We, as a species, find joy in helping others. But Liz couldn't help but wonder if the joy of giving was limited to the relatively trivial amounts of money she used in her research.

Now, on the other end of the line, Chris was telling her about an opportunity she could hardly believe was real. A wealthy couple in the TED community wanted to give ten-thousand-dollar checks away to hundreds of people around the world. Liz's team could track how each person spent this huge windfall and measure how much happiness each purchase provided. And so began what is known as the Mystery Experiment.[34]

On social media, TED invited people in seven countries—including the US, the UK, Kenya, and Indonesia—to sign up for the Mystery Experiment. Rather than revealing that people might get ten thousand dollars, they simply described the experiment as "exciting, surprising, and potentially life-changing." Then, two hundred of the people who signed up received a remarkable email, with a personal video message from Chris Anderson, explaining that they would receive a single transfer of ten thousand dollars. For some participants, especially those in countries like Indonesia, their annual income was effectively doubled overnight. They could spend the windfall in any way they chose. The only catch was that they had to spend all of it within three months, while keeping track of every purchase and completing surveys. And, they were politely asked not to spend the cash on organized crime.

People used the money in all kinds of ways, buying iPhones and washing machines, paying for driving classes and surf lessons, and taking their families to Disney World. But when all the data were in, Liz's team discovered that people reported the highest levels of happiness from making donations to charity. And the average person donated more than sixteen hundred dollars of their windfall to charitable organizations. So, even though the amounts of money involved were orders of magnitude greater than in Liz's original experiments, the picture of humanity that emerged was the same: People derive joy from spending money in generous ways.[35]

This is good news for fighting climate change because it means that donating money to climate organizations can be a source of happiness (to learn about the organizations we're supporting with the proceeds from this book, check out happyclimate.org).

But this doesn't mean that everybody everywhere always experiences pleasure from giving money away. Instead, through years of research, Liz and her team have identified three critical ingredients that turn good deeds into good feelings:

- **Connection:** People are more likely to experience joy from giving if they feel a genuine sense of connection with the people or cause that they're helping.

- **Impact:** Giving is more pleasurable when people can directly observe—or at least vividly imagine—how their generosity is making a difference.

- **Choice:** When people feel like they've been forced to give, they are robbed of the pleasure of generosity, so it's essential that people feel like they have a choice about whether or how to help.

If a coworker corners you in the hallway and asks you to buy a box of cookies to support his kid's Greenpeace fundraiser at school, you might not get much of an emotional boost (unless the cookies are really tasty). But taking the time to find organizations that are doing high-impact work, perhaps in your own community, can amp up the pleasure of giving. Where we live in Vancouver, residents can sponsor a street garden, donating their time or money to turn traffic circles and street corners into beautiful green space.[36] The program is designed to help people meet others in their community, creating a sense of connection, while enabling them to see the impact of their generosity on greening their own neighborhoods.

Of course, sending money farther afield can potentially make a bigger difference, so it's worth looking for high-impact giving opportunities that enable genuine feelings of connection, even at a distance. For our friend Scott Hagan, a chance conversation led to such an opportunity. Scott had spent his career in finance, making plenty of money but feeling a growing sense of boredom and burnout. Then, while attending TED, he not only met Liz, but happened to sit next to a young man from Malawi named William Kamkwamba.

"He didn't know anybody," Scott told us. "And I'm Mr. Party Guy. I'll talk to anybody." As they chatted, Scott learned that William was the subject of a film on Netflix called *The Boy Who Harnessed the Wind*. When William was just a teenager, his village in Malawi had suffered from severe droughts. It was one of many communities in the Global South already feeling the devastating effects of climate change. The village desperately needed a source of power to pump water for their crops. So, at the tender age of thirteen, William read a book about electricity and built a windmill out of spare parts, saving his village. In the years since then, William had garnered international renown, with a book, a TED Talk, and the Netflix film all heralding his story.

Scott was impressed, but he couldn't stop himself from prodding William. "I asked him, 'So what are you going to do now?'" William wasn't sure.

With both of them at a crossroads, they decided to join

forces. Scott donated his money and his project-management skills to build a school in William's home community. Together, Scott and William designed the school so that it would provide not only education but also renewable energy for the community. They covered the school in solar panels, sourced from China. "I don't want this to sound easy. It wasn't easy," Scott told us. "I don't speak Chinese, and I'm trying to buy solar panels in China. It's hard to get them shipped to Africa. And the truck that was driving the solar panels from Tanzania down to Malawi got stuck in the mud."

Not only that, but after everything was installed, Scott realized he had made a mistake in his calculations. He had underestimated the strength of the sun in Malawi, which meant that the school had much more solar power than it needed. "I got the math wrong, and I'm the math guy," Scott confessed. "I got it wrong because the southern hemisphere is different from the northern hemisphere." This turned out to be a wonderful mistake. With the extra power, the school opened up on the weekends as a health clinic and community center for adults. And local entrepreneurs figured out they could capture some of the excess power in small batteries, which they mounted on bicycles to build e-bikes.

As Scott recounted these unexpected ripple effects, he began to tear up. He showed us photos of the children who were getting an international baccalaureate degree at the school. Soon, they could apply to college. And William and his wife, Olivia, are using the solar-powered school as a model, building more than a dozen new schools in other parts of Malawi.

"People have choices in life on where to put their money," he said. "I'm crying telling you this, but there is no end to what can be accomplished." So, rethinking how and where you use your money, from everyday purchases to investments and donations, can help you get more happiness for less carbon—and the ripple effects may be greater than you ever imagined.

The Odyssey of Rush Hour

Commuting is one of the unhappiest daily activities. But in a neighborhood overlooking downtown Portland, Oregon, a gym teacher named Sam Balto turned the rush hour before school into one of the best times of the day. On Earth Day 2022, Coach Balto led a "bike bus," a caravan of children riding their bikes to school together. Seventy-five people joined the caravan. This onetime event became a weekly tradition, rain or shine, with as much as a third of the school participating. As one of the kids explained, "You know it's going to be the highlight of your day. You are going to arrive at school having such a sense of community and joy."

The kids' energy and enthusiasm are contagious. In the houses lining the bike bus route, fans come out and ring cow bells and help to stop traffic. According to one of the dads, being part of the caravan is "like biking in an ocean of joy."

The first bike bus popped up in Brecht, Belgium, in 1998, but in the post-pandemic years, this trend took off, with more than 470 bike buses transporting 32,000 children to school by 2024.[1] Sam was inspired to create the bike bus in his town by videos he saw on social media of the "bicibús" in Barcelona, Spain. Sam, in turn, posted videos that inspired people in other cities to create bike buses (if you want a burst of joy right now, head to happyclimate.org for videos of bike buses and tips on how to start your own).

Sam's story highlights the potential to transform the minutes we spend commuting to school or work—minutes that are typically among our least joyful. In a remarkable study conducted by the US Bureau of Labor Statistics, thirty thousand Americans reported how happy they felt during every activity of their day. Commuting to work ranked dead last.[2]

Part of the problem with commuting is that it undermines our feelings of *time affluence*—the sense that we have enough time to do the things that are important to us. Canadians with long car commutes say that they don't have time for fun anymore and feel trapped in a daily routine. And the more time they spend driving to work, the less time they spend exercising, doing sports, or socializing with friends or family.[3] In a study of two million people in Sweden, individuals who spent more than forty-five minutes commuting to work (each way) were 40 percent more likely to separate from their partner than those with shorter commutes.[4]

In the US, driving accounts for the largest share of the average American's carbon emissions. For a typical driver, commuting produces 3.3 tons of carbon,[5] akin to eating a hamburger for lunch at work five days a week (see chapter 2 for our burger math). Which means that changing how—and how much—we commute is one of the most important sweet spots for enhancing happiness and reducing emissions.

Of course, our individual decisions about commuting are heavily constrained by choices others have made for us. It's tough to walk to work if decades of underfunding have left your city without safe sidewalks. So, rather than insisting that you walk to work, we offer a broad menu of options for rethinking the daily grind. We start with biking, which seems to be the sweetest spot of all and is now much more feasible thanks to the recent revolution in e-bikes. We touch on public transit, and then show how the sharing economy—from Uber to scooters—can help reduce emissions and enhance happiness. Finally, we discuss carpooling and take a deep dive into electric vehicles.

In the second half of the chapter, we consider the potential benefits of cutting back on commuting by working remotely. While digging into some of the least enjoyable minutes of the day, we cover ground that isn't quite as fun as topics like food and fashion. But making changes in how—and whether—you commute could have an even bigger impact on your day-to-day happiness.

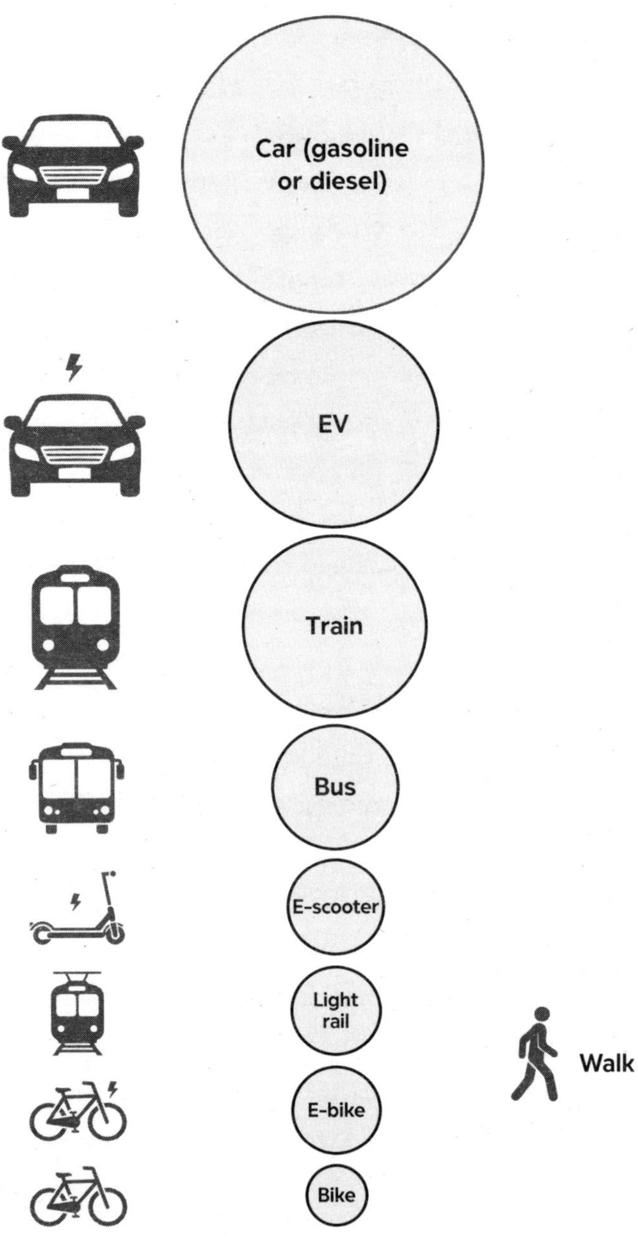

The size of each circle represents the carbon emissions for each mile you travel. Walking is near 0. Adapted from Schunck (2021).[6]

A Biking Renaissance

In studies comparing the emotional consequences of various modes of commuting, biking typically comes out on top. For example, a researcher in Portland, Oregon, surveyed 828 residents and found that cyclists reported the most positive feelings during their commute.[7] The cyclists were closely trailed by a small group of walkers, followed by transit riders. Portland drivers came in dead last—a full point behind cyclists on the researcher's six-point scale of commute well-being. And when more than a million Americans were asked how many days in the past month they had experienced poor mental health, such as stress or depression, those who biked regularly reported fewer.[8]

Meanwhile, a revolution has been unfolding in the world of biking. In 2024, across multiple European countries, the majority of all bikes sold were electric.[9] Although e-bikes are more expensive than traditional bikes, they can pay for themselves by reducing the need to rely on cars. When Americans hop in their cars, they drive fewer than seven miles on most of their trips, a distance that's easy to cover on an e-bike in under twenty minutes.[10] The electric power makes biking accessible to people with health issues or disabilities, for whom biking might have been impractical just a decade ago. Jessica Tillyer, a mom in Montclair, New Jersey, has a large electric cargo bike, which provides plenty of space for hauling around her two kids and all their stuff.[11] And e-bikes eliminate the hassles of searching for parking and waiting in line at school drop-off. The popularity of e-bikes is creating new challenges for cities, though, as these fast-moving vehicles compete for space with pedestrians and drivers.

One solution lies in creating more dedicated bike lanes. In New York City, the Hudson River Greenway now stretches for almost thirteen miles along the West Side of Manhattan, separated from traffic, and seven thousand people cycle it each day—more than any other bikeway in the country.[12] Across the Atlantic, Paris is getting a makeover from its mayor, Anne Hidalgo, who aspires to make every street in the City of Love bikeable.[13] She envisions creating a "15-minute city," in which residents can get everywhere they need to go—to work, school, stores, and entertainment—in fifteen minutes. In just one year, from October 2022 to 2023, cycling in Paris doubled. Car trips have fallen by 50 percent.[14]

Minneapolis might be the Paris of North America. This Midwestern metropolis was ranked among the top large US cities in 2025 for its network of safe and wisely connected bike lanes (by the nonprofit organization PeopleForBikes).[15] Sarah Ryals bought an e-bike to get around the Minneapolis area with her beagle, Ellie, who suffers from separation anxiety. Sarah says, "When people spot the beagle in my basket, ears flapping and nose turned up and sniffing the fresh air, their faces light up with surprise and glee." For Sarah, "the best surprise has been the way the bike builds community. Everyone we pass stops to smile."[16]

As well as creating feelings of connection, commuting by bike can provide an opportunity to squeeze some exercise into a busy day. Some of the best data on this topic comes from a large-scale European study known, delightfully, as PASTA (Physical Activity through Sustainable Transport Approaches).[17] Participants in this study reported how many days per week they got at least thirty minutes of exercise. Those who rode bikes hit the thirty-minute mark on more days per week than those who didn't bike—and this was especially the case for e-bike owners. In fact, even though it takes less effort to pedal an e-bike than a traditional bike, e-bike owners got just as much exercise in total per week because they covered more distance.

Exercise can provide an emotional high, at least for some people. Scientists long thought it stemmed from a rise in endorphins, a hormone that acts on the opioid system (making exercise kind of like free morphine). But this theory hasn't held up so well. Instead, newer research suggests that exercise acts on the endocannabinoid system, so if anything, it might be like free cannabis. To test this idea, researchers gave rats the opportunity to run on a wheel, which they had to poke with their noses to unlock,[18] or to poke another button for nibbles of chocolate. Rats are chocolate lovers, but faced with this choice, many of them chose to poke the exercise wheel—until, that is, the researchers surgically removed the rats' endocannabinoid receptors. Then, the rats lost interest in exercise, gorging themselves on chocolate instead. The researchers speculate that people who get a big emotional boost from exercise might have particularly sensitive endocannabinoid receptors.

There is even a little bit of evidence that exercise can enhance creativity.[19] For example, after doing aerobics, British adults were able to think of more interesting ways to use ordinary objects like cardboard boxes or tin cans. So, biking to work—or walking, if you're lucky enough to live nearby—might help you arrive at the office feeling creative and cheerful.

Public Transit

Studies in North America and Europe show that taking public transit produces low levels of happiness, compared with other ways of getting around. But in China, the government has invested around $100 billion per year to create a high-speed rail network that has transformed daily life for people with long commutes.[20] These trains move at speeds of around two hundred miles per hour—faster than the takeoff speed of an airplane. And the ride is so smooth that YouTube is filled with "coin test" videos, where passengers successfully balance a coin on the windowsill of these superspeed trains. When new high-speed rail stations open in China, overall happiness increases significantly among residents of the surrounding city.[21]

Even taking the subway is relatively pleasant in China's major cities. The subway cars are spacious, clean, safe, and comfortably air-conditioned. They run on time. Children ride them alone. And one study found that the closer people lived to subway stations in Shanghai, the happier they felt.[22]

JZ's parents live in China, and they were stunned when they rode the subway in New York City. It smelled terrible. They saw rats in dark, damp corners of the stations. They felt like they had gone back in time.

A brighter future is now on display in Florida, though. In 2023, a private company opened a train service called Brightline stretching from Orlando to Miami, with six stops along the way. The train is fully electric and reaches speeds of up to 125 miles per hour. Commuters can get from Miami to Fort Lauderdale in thirty-eight minutes—while enjoying Wi-Fi and snacks—whereas driving the same distance can take ninety minutes during rush hour. The train is clean and quiet, and one TikTok creator gushed that it is "the best train in America."

The Joy of Shared Rides

Most cars are parked 95 percent of the time.[23] This level of inefficiency should keep economists up at night. From a climate perspective, it means we are making way, way too many cars—and wasting five to ten tons of carbon a pop. That's where ride-sharing apps like Uber and Lyft come in, along with car-sharing services such as Zipcar and Turo. While ride-sharing services are like modern taxis, car-sharing services are like modern rental cars. So, if you live in a city that offers these services, it's worth considering whether you actually need to own a car.

Uber invited 173 people in seven cities (including Miami, L.A., and Toronto) to experiment with giving up their car for one month.[24] When you account for insurance, maintenance, gas, and so on, people spend an average of a thousand dollars per month to operate their own car. So, Uber gave each participant one thousand dollars in "transportation credits," which they could use for ride-sharing, scooters, and bikes through the Uber platform, as well as public transit. It took participants a couple of weeks to adapt, but by the end of the study, 20 percent of them said they were likely to give up their car for good. Some of them described improvements to their physical and mental health. According to Uber's report, participants mentioned feeling "a greater sense of community, a deeper connection to their neighborhoods, and an increased interest in exploring new areas."

If ride-sharing or car-sharing enables you to give up your own car, then it can put a major dent in your personal emissions. But it's not so great when solo riders choose to hop in a big, gas-guzzling Uber rather than walking, biking, or busing through downtown, and as of April 2024, about 90 percent of Uber rides were in gas vehicles in North America and Europe.[25] The company has promised that all rides will be in zero-emission vehicles by 2040.[26]

Although that feels like a long way off, in most North American cities, you can already choose an electric or hybrid car by scrolling down and selecting the "Uber Green" option. And every time you do so, you're not only cutting your own carbon emissions—you're also sending a message that riders prefer EVs. You might consider an extra tip for the driver who chose to invest in an electric car. Your fellow riders are already doing this. According to Lyft, EV drivers earned 20 percent more in tips than drivers of gas cars, across the US.[27]

The sharing economy is also embracing "micromobility" options, including bikes, e-bikes, and electric scooters.[28] When Liz took her family to Paris, her son, Oliver, declared that the best part of the whole trip was riding an e-scooter along the Seine. E-scooters are a low-carbon option for getting around, generating emissions similar to taking light rail. But these scooters have spurred controversy and even bans in some cities. Shortly after Liz got home from Paris, the city banned e-scooters due to pedestrian complaints, safety concerns, and the unsightly appearance of scooters scattered around sidewalks. It's worth figuring out how to make e-scooters fit into city life. Not only are they fun to ride, but they can help to solve the "last mile" problem by getting people from a central train station to their own front door.

Liz witnessed the newest vision of urban transportation during a visit to San Francisco in the summer of 2024. She was stunned to see people climb into the back seat of a white electric Jaguar, which took off down the street with no one in the driver's seat. The steering wheel turned on its own, as though operated by a ghost. Squinting to get a closer look, Liz saw that the car was a Waymo One, part of an autonomous ride-sharing service being rolled out by Alphabet (Google's parent company). The car was topped with elaborate spinning cameras, allowing it to navigate the chaotic streets of San Francisco.

As Liz watched the car drive away, something even more surprising happened: The car came to a full and complete stop at a crosswalk, giving pedestrians plenty of time to make their way across the street. In San Francisco and other cities, drivers commonly race through crosswalks and barely pause at stop signs, endangering pedestrians and bikers. California's streets are the third-deadliest in the country for pedestrians. According to Jonathan Adkins, the CEO of the Governors Highway Safety Association, "Nationally, pedestrian deaths are the highest they've been since 1981. That's kind of crazy because our vehicles are safer."[29]

While drivers are accustomed to bending the rules, Waymo vehicles are programmed to follow traffic laws, halting at stop signs and driving within the speed limit.[30] According to the AAA Foundation for Traffic Safety, pedestrians are five times more likely to be killed if they are struck by a vehicle going forty-two miles per hour versus twenty-five. So, taking a Waymo might not only lower your personal emissions but also make it safer for everyone around you to choose active, low-carbon options like walking and biking.

Carpooling

In Uber's study, some participants—particularly in the suburbs—embraced an alternative that many people overlook: good old-fashioned carpooling. By the end of the study, 64 percent of them said they would carpool more often going forward.

Driving two of your friends, rather than driving alone, cuts carbon by as much as taking the commuter rail. Driving four of your friends reduces your carbon footprint by the same amount as riding a crowded city bus. And while spending time commuting ranks among the worst activities of the day for happiness, socializing ranks among the very best. So, turning a lonely commute into an opportunity to catch up with friends can transform some of the worst minutes of the day into some of the best.

Louise Stephen, who lives in Edinburgh, Scotland, wanted to carpool but didn't have any friends with compatible commutes. She used Liftshare, one of many apps that are like OkCupid for commuting. As Louise explains, "I was thinking about the environmental impact of so many empty cars, but I was also thinking how mind-numbingly bored I was. So I thought it would be good to start sharing the journey with someone else."[31] She matched with a woman named Cara Jardine, who had a similar commute. Louise and Cara talk about politics, podcasts, and running, and Cara says, "We've become good friends."

When five thousand Dutch people were asked to rate their happiness throughout the day, they consistently reported lower happiness while they were commuting than while they were hanging out at home—with one exception.[32] Commuting with other people actually provided more happiness than being at home. Commuting with others even beat out biking (and in the bike mecca of the Netherlands, no less!). While finding someone to share the commute can feel like a lot of effort, the rewards—for both climate and happiness—are worth it.

Electric Vehicles Are Charged with Joy

Over 90 percent of Americans own a car, so giving it up can seem unfathomable. But electric vehicles provide an enjoyable, low-carbon alternative to traditional gas cars. Mike Murphy—a

Republican political strategist who has advised Arnold Schwarzenegger, Jeb Bush, and Mitt Romney—bought an EV when gas prices soared past five dollars per gallon. "And I found I love the damn thing. Just love it," he says. "It is pure joy to glide by a service station these days."

In the summer of 2023, he decided to drive from his home in New Hampshire to Los Angeles in his EV (a Volkswagen ID.4).[33] "The whole drive an EV across the country caper struck my friends in New Hampshire as complete insanity," he explained. "To them, the rules were clear: *trustworthy cars run on gas dammit, not e-magic! This isn't . . . Europe!!!*" But he was determined to prove his friends wrong. He covered six hundred miles per day, stretching his legs and exploring while his car juiced up at charging stations. Meanwhile, he got to "enjoy the one last untaxed pleasure left to most Americans, as cheap or free electricity filled up my battery. . . . Due to the free fast charging that came with my VW, I think my total e-fuel cost was about $35."

Murphy started the EV Politics Project to tackle what he sees as "EV bashing" within his own party. Rather than touting the potentially divisive "save the planet" tagline, Murphy argues that EV supporters must "focus on the vehicle: Fast, fun, no gas. Less regular maintenance needs. All of these attributes are big winners with Republican consumers. Why? They focus on the driving experience, not political issues."[34]

Around the world, the success of EVs has hinged on providing a genuinely pleasurable driving experience. In Norway, the government introduced a cornucopia of policies to promote EV adoption, beginning in the 1990s. They offered major tax incentives, free tolls, and free parking for EV buyers. Nothing worked. Finally, in 2013, EV adoption shot upward. Why? The Tesla Model S had arrived in Norway.[35] The expert car review site Edmunds described this car as "sleek, seductive, luxurious, powerful and inspiring." These are not words that come to mind in describing the earlier generation of EVs. Now nearly every car manufacturer offers EVs that are fun to drive.

But would buying an EV really make a dent in your personal carbon emissions? The short answer is a resounding yes. But the size of this dent depends on where you live. In West Virginia, nine out of the ten largest power plants run on coal—so, even electric vehicles rely on coal.[36] Thanks to the efficiency of electric engines, though, driving an EV still provides a 31 percent reduction in emissions. But you would get a 94 percent reduction in emissions if you lived in the state with the cleanest energy: the Green Mountain state of Vermont, which relies primarily on hydroelectric power. (To see current stats for all fifty states, visit happyclimate.org.)

In deciding whether to buy an EV, it's also worth considering how much you drive. Liz always assumed that JZ drove an electric car, given her passionate advocacy around climate change. So, she was surprised when JZ picked her up in a gaspowered Honda Fit. Liz was even more surprised to climb in the car and discover that it lacked power locks, power steering, or anything resembling a modern car stereo system. JZ had purchased the car a decade earlier, as a graduate student. In all that time, she had still put fewer than fifty thousand miles on it because she lives downtown and walks almost everywhere. Even though she can now afford to upgrade, JZ opted to stick with her antique Honda Fit. After all, just making a new electric vehicle generates almost nine tons of carbon—even more than making a new gas car, which generates around six tons on average.[37]

If you're ready to spring for an EV, though, the best strategy may be to buy used rather than new. EVs depreciate in value faster than gas cars, losing as much as half their value in their first year, in part because the speed of innovation drives up demand for the newest models.[38] But this is good news for many people, given that the high cost of EVs is a major barrier to buying one. So, an EV that is one or two years old can give you access to recent technology at a substantially reduced price.

If you really want to buy a new car, then choosing an EV over a gas car will "pay for itself," in terms of carbon, after about fifteen thousand miles on average.[39] This works out to about a year of driving for the typical American. And in a clean-energy state like Vermont, your hydro-powered EV will reach "carbon parity" with a gas car after only around six months (it'll take more like five years in West Virginia).

Over longer periods of time, the benefits of EVs really add up: Shifting from a gas car to an EV saves about as much carbon as not owning a car at all (across the lifetime of the car).[40] This is because even people who don't own cars end up burning gas through ride-shares and car rentals. And, according to the American Lung Association, transitioning to a country of clean energy and EVs would eliminate almost three million asthma attacks among American children by 2050, alongside many other health benefits.[41]

Gretchen Goldman, who helped to implement the Inflation Reduction Act in the US Department of Transportation, has seen a glimpse of this future. She drives an electric car, but she rented a gas-powered camper for a family vacation. When her family stopped at a gas station to fuel up, her young son wrinkled his nose at the unpleasant—and unfamiliar—smell. She realized he had never smelled gas before. It may not be long before all children are so lucky. In only six years, from 2018 to 2024, the percentage of new cars with electric (vs. gas) engines skyrocketed from just 2 percent to 22 percent around the world. And by 2025, 97 percent of new cars in Norway were electric.[42]

The Speed & Scale project tracks global progress on key dimensions for cutting emissions, and mostly it's kind of depressing—as of 2025, we were failing or hitting "code red" in areas like reducing food waste, cutting back on methane, and moving toward sustainable aviation fuels. But when it comes to electric cars, the world is on track. And the approach that's worked for EVs provides a model for the rest of the climate movement: Instead of asking people to make sacrifices in order to reduce carbon, offer alternatives that actually enhance their everyday pleasure.

Ditching the Office

Rather than changing *how* you commute to work, it's worth considering whether you could eliminate this joy-sucking, carbon-intensive activity entirely. By working remotely five days per

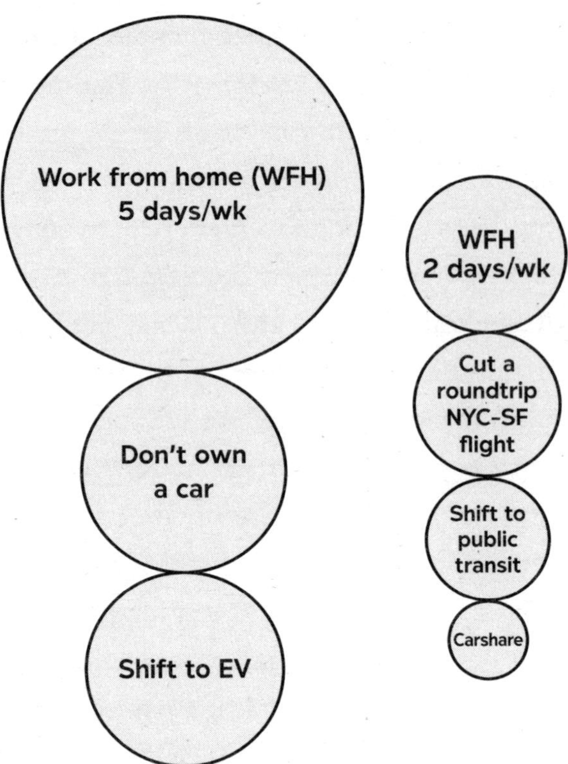

The size of each circle represents the relative carbon savings from various lifestyle changes. Adapted from Ivanova et al. (2020).[43]

week, the average American would cut their total emissions in half.[44] And even working from home twice per week could cut emissions by more than 10 percent.

Of course, many people—including our society's most essential workers—have no choice but to show up in person every day for their jobs. But if you're lucky enough to have some control over whether you work from home some or all of the time, then it's worth taking a close look at recent research, which reveals when and for whom remote work enhances well-being. And one positive ripple effect of the COVID-19 pandemic is that some employers who would never have considered allowing remote work may now be open to it.

Even before the pandemic, opportunities to work from home were rising steadily, buoyed by technological innovations in communication, like Zoom and Slack. By 2019, Americans worked from home about 5 percent of the time. This figure sky-rocketed during the pandemic, before leveling off at about 30 percent in 2024—equivalent to around forty years of pre-pandemic growth![45]

Not everyone was thrilled with this whirlwind change. In 2022, Elon Musk told his employees at Tesla that they had to be in the office at least forty hours per week, adding, "If you don't show up, we will assume you have resigned." And this requirement applied not only to those on the factory floor, but to managers, finance folks, and others who may have felt that they could do their jobs perfectly well from home, with just a laptop.

In a subsequent interview with CNBC, Musk lamented, "The laptop class is living in la-la land." Musk explained, "I'm a big believer that people are more productive when they are in person."

But we don't have to rely on beliefs—Elon Musk's or anyone else's—because we've got science. Studying the consequences of working from home is a little tricky, though, because individuals who choose to work from home might differ in lots of ways from those who choose to go to the office. Indeed, research suggests that less industrious individuals may be especially likely to choose a remote option, allowing them to "shirk from home."

So, if we want to know whether working remotely *causes* lower productivity—rather than vice versa—we really need to randomly assign people to work from home or from the office. And back in 2010, a large company in China decided to do exactly this.[46] One of the largest digital travel agencies in the world asked its call center employees in Shanghai whether they would be interested in coming to the office just once per week, and working from home on the other four days.

About half the employees volunteered. Then, in dramatic fashion, the CEO drew a ping-pong ball from an urn.[47] The ball read, "Even." So, volunteers with even birthdays (e.g., November 2) were assigned to work from home four days per week for the next nine months. Meanwhile, their colleagues with odd birthdays had to keep coming into the office every day.

Leaders of the company hoped that performance wouldn't plunge among those assigned to work from home. But because the cost of office space was sky-high in Shanghai, the leadership was willing to sacrifice some degree of productivity. To their surprise, however, performance didn't plummet; instead, it improved dramatically. While working from home, employees took fewer breaks and made more calls per minute, leading to a 13 percent improvement in performance overall across the nine-month experiment.

From our perspective, though, what's even more interesting is how employees *felt*. Compared with those who came into the office every day, those who got to work from home reported experiencing more positive moods during the workday and feeling more satisfied with their jobs. They were less likely to agree with depressing statements like "I feel burned out from my work" and "I dread getting up in the morning and having to face another day on the job." They were 50 percent less likely to quit. Most remarkably, they felt more satisfied with their lives as a whole.

Why? Before the experiment, the average call center employee sank 80 minutes per day into commuting. So, when they got the chance to work from home, these 80 minutes were returned to them. Sixty-five percent of employees said they used their newfound time to get more sleep, and 55 percent reported spending more time with family.

Social Costs of Remote Work

From everything we've said so far, it seems like working from home is an easy win—and that's what the travel agency's senior management concluded. They decided to offer the work-from-home option permanently. But at this point, half the employees who had won the ping-pong-ball lottery decided to return to the office. How come? Many of them reported feeling lonely at home. What's interesting is that all of them had put their hands up nine months earlier when asked if they would like to work from home, suggesting they didn't anticipate loneliness would be a big concern. This study was conducted before the pandemic, but many of us now know how lonely remote work can feel.

Loneliness isn't the only social cost of remote work. Missing out on in-person contact at the office can undermine long-term career success. In particular, junior people get less feedback when they're not in the same building as their senior colleagues. This insight comes from a remarkable study conducted with software engineers on the campus of a Fortune 500 company, shortly before the pandemic.[48] The campus included two buildings a few blocks apart. Some teams were co-located in a single building, and these teams typically met in person each day. Other teams were spread across the two buildings. They could have walked a few blocks to get together. But why walk when you can Zoom? So, they operated like remote teams, hopping online for brief check-ins.

There's some evidence that moving meetings online made the cross-building teams more efficient in the short term. This efficiency came at a cost, however. Junior engineers on these teams were less likely to ask for and receive feedback from their senior colleagues. And these effects were especially pronounced for women. The female engineers who were in the same building as the rest of their team received 40 percent more feedback than those who were separated from their colleagues. In particular, these women were much more likely to ask for clarification and pose follow-up questions.

Of course, feedback isn't free. Having time away from their junior colleagues benefited senior engineers. This was especially true for women, who sank more time into mentoring when they were seated with their colleagues, reducing the amount of code they wrote.

When the pandemic hit, both buildings shut down. Although the stress of the pandemic dragged down everyone's performance, senior engineers who were no longer surrounded by their colleagues showed a relative benefit: Now that they weren't spending so much time mentoring, they could write more lines of code.

Meanwhile, at other companies, leaders picked up on a similar pattern. In May 2020, after Meta's employees began working from home as a result of the pandemic, CEO Mark Zuckerberg noted that "a lot of people are actually saying that they're more productive now."[49] He predicted that half his employees would be working remotely in five to ten years, while vowing, "We're going to be the most forward-leaning company on remote work at our scale."

But the follow-up data from the study of the two-building engineering campus contained a cautionary tale. Over time, after both buildings had shut down due to the pandemic, the mentorship that junior engineers on single-building teams had received began to pay off. The junior engineers who had been trained by colleagues in the same building produced more output and were more likely to get pay raises than their peers from two-building teams. Even though everyone was stuck at home, working on their own, the previous experience of in-person mentorship mattered.

Three years after envisioning a remote work future for Meta, in March 2023, Mark Zuckerberg wrote a memo to Meta employees articulating a very different vision. He described company data showing that junior engineers performed better when they worked in person with teammates at least three days per week. Even though Meta was in the business of creating closeness online, he wrote, "it is still easier to build trust in person," and "those relationships help us work more effectively." So, he told his employees, "I encourage all of you to find more opportunities to work with your colleagues in person." In fact, he did more than encourage them; he required that almost all employees be back in the office at least three days a week by September.

While Meta doesn't share its performance data, we can get a window into one key challenge of remote work from a study of twenty million scientific articles.[50] This study showed that early-career folks are given different types of work to do when they're remote. Specifically, when less established team members aren't in the same place as their collaborators, they are given technical tasks to complete, like running data analyses. But when these junior team members are on-site, they get more involved in conceiving new ideas. The authors argue that "on-site teams are particularly important as they serve as an escalator for new talent to co-lead in conceptualizing the next breakthrough."

The costs of remote work have not gone unnoticed by young people. Among Americans who worked from home during the pandemic, those aged twenty to twenty-nine were least likely to say they would want full-time remote work.[51] So, if you're just starting your career, it's probably worth commuting to the office at least some of the time.

Working in the Sweet Spot

If there are real costs to working remotely, when and how often should you head into the office? The answers hinge on the kind of work you do, and the life you lead, but several studies can help you find your own sweet spot.

One of the biggest questions is how often you need to bother commuting to work to reap the benefits of in-person connection. A landmark study points to the value of spending three days a week in the office. In 2021, the same large digital travel agency that had assigned its call-center employees to hybrid work a decade earlier ran an experiment with sixteen hundred employees across marketing, engineering, and finance.[52] They randomly assigned these employees to either come into the office five days per week or work from home on Wednesdays and Fridays. Compared with their colleagues who were coming into the office every day, the hybrid workers reported significantly greater work-life balance and job satisfaction. Most remarkably, they reported higher overall *life* satisfaction—the core component of happiness that's hardest to change. Meanwhile, their performance reviews were unaffected, even on social dimensions like communication and leadership.

While this study shows that spending three days in the office is enough, another experiment suggests that spending only two days in the office might be even better.[53] A major NGO in Bangladesh randomly assigned 108 of its employees to come into the office a lot (more than 40 percent of the time), a moderate amount (around 20 to 40 percent of the time), or just a little (up to 20 percent of the time). Compared with their colleagues who came into the office a lot or a little, those assigned to come in a moderate amount—about twice per week in a typical five-day workweek—seemed to flourish. They created more new connections with colleagues, and their emails contained more positive sentiments and novel ideas. They reported the lowest levels of isolation and the best work-life balance, as well as the highest overall satisfaction with working from home.

If you have some control over how many days to go into the office—or you're choosing between jobs with different requirements for in-person work—it's worth thinking about how much time you would get back by working from home. Individuals with long commutes consistently show the biggest benefits from working from home, so if you're lucky enough to live a fifteen-minute bike ride away from your job, then working from home probably won't buy you much in terms of happiness or carbon savings. That said, working from home also saves time on what scientists call "grooming." When people work from home, they are less likely to shower, shave, put on makeup, or even brush their teeth (ew!). Several studies find that working from home benefits women more than men,[54] and we would speculate that this difference might stem in part from the time savings women reap from reduced pressure to look good at the office.

Given all this individual variability, it's tempting to conclude that organizations should just let employees choose when and how often to come into the office. But research suggests that this is a terrible idea.[55] When even one team member is remote, their absence affects the way the rest of the team interacts with one another. Teams move meetings online to accommodate their remote members, which can mean that people commute to work only to end up spending their day on Zoom. As a result, those who do come in may not reap the full benefits of being together in person. Not only that, an individual's decision to work from home may create a domino effect, reducing everyone's motivation to come into the office.

We experienced a version of this domino effect firsthand in the wake of the pandemic. To accommodate a handful of faculty members who had lingering concerns about COVID-19, our department allowed all of us to attend monthly faculty meetings in person or over Zoom, long after our campus reopened. The thing you need to know about faculty meetings is that they are very, very boring. So, on an individual level, it always seemed more enjoyable to Zoom in. Between the two of us, we have folded laundry, showered, shopped for groceries, cleaned bunny litter, and downhill skied, all while Zooming in to faculty meetings. While this kind of multitasking can feel productive on an individual level, it comes at a cost to the group.

Faculty meetings can actually be pretty important—they're the one time when all the professors in a department get together to solve organizational challenges. As the months passed, with most faculty members choosing to Zoom in, we noticed that these meetings became more contentious. Back when everyone had come to faculty meetings in person, an essential part of the meetings took place in the hallways before and afterward, as pairs and small groups chatted about the thorniest challenges on the agenda. These casual hallway conversations relieved tensions, smoothed ruffled feathers, and helped everyone understand one another. Zoom doesn't have hallways.

Not all meetings need to be in person, though—and some might even be better online. To examine this idea, a large telecommunications company randomly assigned almost fifteen hundred employees to collaborate in pairs, either in person or via video call.[56] The pairs first spent an hour generating ideas for new products, and then selected a single idea to propose to the company. Compared with pairs who worked together in person, the video callers generated fewer creative ideas. But when it came to the more analytic task of selecting the single best idea, the pairs who met over video did just as well as—or even better than—those who met in person. In-person meetings may be especially valuable for creative brainstorming, but videoconferencing may promote a narrower focus that's actually helpful for analytic tasks.

The key, then, is for individuals and organizations to be intentional about the kinds of activities that are completed in person versus remotely. No one should have to drive for forty-five minutes to sit in an office for eight hours of Zoom meetings. Jose Barrero, one of the pioneers of research on working from home, says that organizations should enable employees to "see the value of coming in . . . if there's going to be a team meeting, and interacting in person, and having lunch together, it's a much easier case to make than if you're just asking them to come in for free doughnuts at nine a.m."[57]

But before denigrating free doughnuts, we should note that the privilege of being able to work from home is disproportionately available to well-educated individuals. Most people still have to show up for their jobs (and may not even be offered doughnuts!). If you have the privilege of choosing whether or how often to work from home, here are some questions to consider to identify your own personal sweet spot:

- How long and painful is your commute?

- How much "grooming" time could you save by working from home?

- Does your daily life outside of work offer plentiful opportunities for social interaction?

- How important is it for you to receive (or give) mentorship at this stage of your career?

- How much teamwork or collaboration does your role at work require?

- Do you enjoy being able to focus on your own work without disruptions?

Going Extremely Remote

While remote and hybrid employees typically live within driving distance of their workplace, some organizations now offer a *work-from-anywhere* option, giving employees almost total geographic flexibility. When the US Patent and Trademark Office offered a work-from-anywhere option to employees, those who chose to take it showed a spike in productivity, worth more than $130 million to the organization.[58] Importantly, these employees were reviewing patent applications on their own, so they didn't need to engage in much collaboration. And they had already spent at least two years working in the office, and some time working from home, so they were well equipped for remote work.

Although the government didn't collect information on employees' happiness, interviews with the employees highlight the potential benefits of this policy. Some employees moved closer to their extended families. One of them explained that the move meant her children get to spend time with their grandparents and play with their cousins: "Being closer to family has improved my overall happiness because we are able to spend time together on all holidays rather than just the major ones." Indeed, the emotional benefits of living near extended family may outweigh the costs of missing out on interactions with colleagues.

In 2022, Airbnb announced a new policy that sought to offer both geographic flexibility *and* a sense of community among coworkers. The company's CEO, Brian Chesky, explained, "Airbnb is in the business of human connection above all else, and we believe that the most meaningful connections happen in person. Zoom is great for maintaining relationships, but it's not the best way to deepen them. Additionally, some creative work and collaboration is best done when you're in the same room."

Chesky told employees, "Instead of spending a set number

of days in the office together, we're prioritizing meaningful in-person gatherings that will happen throughout the year." Most employees could live wherever they wanted, but they would be asked to get together for a week or so, about four times per year.

From our perspective, Airbnb's policy looks like it might be a win for happiness, to the extent that it enables people to live in a place they love, while still fostering meaningful social connections with colleagues at quarterly gatherings. But is this policy a win for the climate? As we'll discuss in chapter 5, flying is terrible for climate change. Driving to work every day is really bad, too, though. If we assume the average American burns 3.3 tons of carbon per year by driving a gas-powered car to work, then replacing all this driving with quarterly flights might actually be better. Airbnb enables employees to convene at their nearest "Ground Control" office. So an employee who chose to live by the beach in Miami would burn only around half a ton of carbon by taking direct flights to Airbnb's Atlanta office quarterly—thereby saving more than 2.5 tons of carbon compared with the typical daily car commute.

Living in a remote location that doesn't offer a direct flight to the office undercuts these savings but doesn't completely erase them. For example, living in Duluth, Minnesota, and flying through Chicago to Airbnb's NYC office would still save almost a ton of carbon annually. So, while we would love to see more rigorous research on work-from-anywhere policies, we are excited about this increasingly popular strategy for maximizing happiness and minimizing carbon.

Work Less

Instead of going into the office several days per week and working from home on the other days, it's also worth considering whether you could go into the office some days and simply *not work* on the other days. For many of us who are accustomed to working forty hours or more per week, it's hard to imagine a different lifestyle. But let's try to envision alternative realities—if only to consider what could be possible in the future. After all, the forty-hour workweek is itself a fairly recent invention. In the early 1900s, most Americans worked twelve to fourteen hours per day.[59] Then, in 1926, Henry Ford replaced the typical forty-eight-hour workweek in his factories with a forty-hour week, after recognizing that this cut in hours barely affected total productivity. Almost fifteen years later, the US government passed a law limiting the standard workweek to forty hours. Canada, Australia, and other countries followed suit, catching up with the many European countries that had already instituted similar limits. Over the past one hundred years, working hours have fallen by about 20 percent around the world.[60]

Reducing work hours further would be a win for the climate, although estimating the magnitude of this win is tricky. In 2021, a British nonprofit called Platform London issued a report arguing that moving to a four-day workweek would cut emissions by 21 percent.[61] This statistic was picked up by the media and cited in government reports. But it's probably wrong. In essence, the report assumes that if people aren't working, they will just stay home and maybe read, meditate, or garden—emitting zero carbon in the process.

In reality, though, people are likely to use their newfound time for enjoyable activities outside the home, including travel—especially if they get a three-day weekend. Still, a four-day workweek should provide a meaningful reduction in carbon, especially if companies shut down their offices (and all their carbon-sucking equipment) for the remaining three days.

And the four-day workweek may be an idea whose time has come. Beginning in 2022, the nonprofit 4 Day Week Global invited companies to participate in an innovative six-month trial.[62] The companies had to substantially reduce employees' work hours—without reducing their pay. Thirty-three companies signed on, offering reduced work hours to more than nine hundred of their employees across the US, Australia, Ireland, and other countries. Although companies could choose exactly how to reduce work hours, almost all of them adopted the four-day workweek.

The trial produced stunningly positive results for happiness. Employees' overall satisfaction with their lives went up by almost a full point on a ten-point scale. Their positive emotions increased, and their negative emotions decreased. Job satisfaction rose. The biggest change, not surprisingly, appeared in their satisfaction with the amount of time they had to do things they liked.

Meanwhile, most of the organizations reported that instituting reduced work hours had yielded positive effects, even for overall productivity. Almost all of them planned to keep the reduction in work time after the six-month trial ended. This finding suggests that it may be essential for companies to experiment with shorter working hours in order to overcome the deep-seated assumption that less work time equals less productivity.

Indeed, a subsequent trial with sixty-one organizations and twenty-nine hundred workers in the UK produced similarly positive results.[63] As the CEO of one organization put it, "You're looking at giving people 40, 50 extra days a year, which is incredible really. . . . If we can make it work, it's very precious."

Of course, employees may have said they felt happier in part because they recognized that their company had provided them with a valuable gift—so, reporting dissatisfaction would be like looking a gift horse in the mouth. In the trials, there was no comparison group of employees who received a different type of gift, like a salary raise or other benefit, instead of a free day. And we also don't know how long the happiness benefits will last. It's possible that having Friday off confers a newfound sense of time affluence, but that people quickly fill up their Fridays with new activities that leave them feeling just as busy as before. That said, for business leaders, instituting a four-day workweek could be an innovative sweet spot for increasing employee happiness and cutting carbon.

Fly Less

Ben Sommers, a sales executive in the Bay Area, used to spend his days crisscrossing the country for business meetings. He told us, "It was expected that I would travel across the country for a thirty-minute in-person meeting. With a six-hour flight each way. I lost so much time."[64] Many people don't need to fly for work, but those like Ben have an outsize carbon impact.

The pandemic provided an opportunity for frequent fliers to rethink their approach to business travel. Ben explains, "The other day, I was talking with a potential partner in Michigan. I said that I grew up in Michigan, and I would be happy to fly there and meet up in person. But this guy told me he doesn't even go into the office—he just works from home." So, Ben says, he didn't book a flight because "I'm not going to go to his house."

His wife, Nita Sommers, a healthcare executive, began her career in consulting, working with companies around the country. She says, "When I was in consulting, the expectation was that you would fly to be on-site Monday to Thursday." But in the wake of the pandemic, "a lot of people just don't want that anymore. It was expensive, and now they've figured out hybrid ways to be on-site." And when it comes to deciding whether to fly across the country for an in-person meeting, Nita says, "it's more acceptable to do the calculus on whether both the time and money investment is worth the extra added value." And that calculus should include carbon, too. Eliminating just one round-trip flight from San Francisco to New York City would save as much carbon as working from home two days per week for a whole year.

So, when it comes to work travel, it's worth thinking critically about the *return on emissions* that flights offer. While flying less has reduced Ben's carbon emissions and increased his feelings of time affluence, he also recognizes the costs of staying home. "Having the personal connection during those in-person meetings, it was actually meaningful. I could build relationships." So, in choosing whether to fly, it's worth prioritizing the social connections that will matter most to you over the long term.

It can be easy to assume that long-distance travel is essential to building a career. For example, as academics, we took it on faith that traveling around the world giving talks on our research was necessary. That way, other scholars would see our new findings and mention them in their own work, thereby garnering citations for us—basically, academic gold.

But a new study of fifty-five thousand presentations at economics conferences made us rethink our assumptions.[65] The study found that scholars traveled a total of 250 million miles to present these papers. To our surprise, the distance they traveled to present their work had no bearing on how much their papers ended up getting cited. In fact, papers that never got cited—ever, by anyone—generated forty million miles of travel.

The sheer *number* of trips people made to present a paper did seem to make a difference, though: The more times scholars presented a paper, the more it got cited—but for most scholars, presenting the paper nearby was just as good as going far afield.

The thing about economists is that they're willing to do the math to figure out just how much carbon they're squandering. But across many industries, we suspect that people take a lot of flights that offer little return on emissions. These sobering statistics provide an important wake-up call for other fields and industries to question long-held assumptions about the value of business travel.

Our Takeaway

There has never been a better time for questioning assumptions about where and how we work. By throwing the entire world of work into chaos, the pandemic made it acceptable to experiment with new approaches and ask whether the way things had always been done was really the *best* way.

Of course, there is no single approach that works best for everyone. If you're just starting your career and would benefit from being surrounded by colleagues, or you're an essential worker who has no choice but to show up for work, then buying an e-bike or EV could be the optimal sweet spot. On the other hand if you live in a rural area fifty miles from your office and can't afford a new car, then your best bet might be to create a carpool or consider whether and how often you could work from home.

What if quitting your job or moving someplace else is the only way to escape the daily grind of miserable, high-carbon commuting? For readers who are ready to shake up their lives— or at least fantasize about doing so—we turn to major life changes in the penultimate chapter. But first, let's take a break from the daily grind and talk about vacation.

Oh, the Places You'll Go

Eva is a working mother who exudes energy and puts her environmental values into action by cooking elaborate vegetarian meals for her family. Her partner, Ara, does most of the shopping, and when he occasionally forgets to bring a reusable bag, Eva admits that she goes ballistic. With a laugh, Ara explains, "I come home with some plastic shopping bags and I'm in huge trouble. But, while I was out shopping, Eva bought flights to Europe for a family vacation."

Like Eva, many people who care about climate change—and even many sustainability experts themselves—struggle when it comes to cutting back on vacation travel. When we spoke to a leading sustainability researcher, Xavier Font, he was in the midst of searching for vacation flights. He explained, "Many of us say to ourselves, 'I have been a really nice person for fifty weeks of the year. I'm now going on holiday. Just back off. I feel guilty a lot of the time. Please, could I just have a break from my responsibilities to the planet, to everybody?'"

In fact, individuals who exhibit higher levels of commitment to sustainability at home—by composting, buying organic, and cutting back on energy—actually fly farther and more frequently for vacation.[1] And it's natural to make trade-offs. We can't be perfect all the time. As Xavier puts it, "Many of us say, 'Well, I don't drink alcohol Monday to Friday, but then I allow myself to be a bit naughty on the weekend.' So, the same happens here." But the problem is that recycling all year and then flying to Europe is like teetotaling on weekdays and then doing twenty shots of tequila over the weekend. Indeed, a vegan who flies from New York to Thailand for Christmas will end up with the same carbon footprint as someone who eats meat all year but stays home for the holidays.

Meanwhile, devotees of happiness research have come to value experiences over things. And for good reason. Study after study shows that people get more happiness from buying experiences, including vacation travel, than from buying material things.[2] And an analysis of data from more than two hundred thousand Americans revealed that individuals who made time for vacation were happier, even after accounting for income and working hours.[3]

So, how can people enjoy vacation travel while still minimizing their emissions? To be honest, we felt stumped on this question—and we kept putting off writing this chapter. But as we dug deeper into the research, we found many delightful routes to dealing with this carbon conundrum.

We'll start by mapping out the approaches that most dramatically cut carbon, and then zoom out to consider how to maximize your happiness-to-carbon ratio wherever you go in the world.

Explore Closer to Home

To figure out how to get the most happiness out of a vacation while burning the least carbon, it's helpful to understand when and why tourism provides joy. In exploring this topic, Jeroen Nawijn visited the most popular attractions in Amsterdam and other Dutch cities and asked nearly five hundred tourists how happy they were feeling that day.[4] He grouped their activities into categories such as visiting a museum, shopping, relaxing, traveling, and drinking and doing drugs (after all, this was the Netherlands!). Remarkably, people felt pretty happy regardless of what they were doing—with one notable exception: Tourists reported significantly lower happiness on days when their main activity involved traveling. So, exploring tourist attractions close to home may boost happiness while minimizing the unpleasantness of devoting a precious vacation day to getting there.

And yet, many people never get around to visiting the popular attractions in their hometowns. One small study found that people who had lived in London for a year had been to fewer landmarks, from Kensington Palace to Tower Bridge, than tourists who had spent two weeks there.[5] In fact, the majority of London residents had seen fewer landmarks in their own city than in other cities they had visited. A similar study with former Chicago residents found that they had visited relatively few landmarks in the Windy City—until they were about to move away. So, ironically, the fact that tourist attractions in our hometowns are always available may make us less likely to visit them.[6]

It could be that visiting nearby tourist attractions just feels humdrum. But the former Chicago residents reported enjoying themselves very much when they bothered to take an architectural boat tour of their city, explore Shedd Aquarium, or spend time at other attractions that bring people to Chicago. So, if you live in a place that draws lots of tourists, turning yourself into a hometown tourist may be a big win for low-carbon happiness.

Beyond museums and monuments, people often seek out travel for the chance to experience new cuisines. But again, we may overlook opportunities for culinary exploration closer to home. "I find it really sad that I might travel to India to learn to cook with a local family there," Xavier told us, "even though my next-door neighbor—and I'm not even joking—he's from India. I don't even know his name. I didn't have to travel that far to go and learn how to cook a chapati. I just had to get to know my neighbor and offer him a cup of tea."

Our friend Jennifer Tackett took this idea to heart when the opportunity to travel ground to a halt during the COVID-19 pandemic. "My kids and I *love* to travel," she said, "and having to stop so suddenly was really hard on us." As one trip after another got canceled, Jennifer decided to start a new family tradition: Travel Tuesday. Each family member took turns picking a country they wanted to visit. "Over Tuesday night dinner, we would learn more about the place. We would plan out what we would do there and where we would stay." Jennifer loves to cook, so she would dive into research and make a meal that brought the place to life in their dining room.

She shared each experience on Facebook, where we drooled over her culinary tourism. "Sometimes I research a country and pick something outside-the-box. Other times I focus on street food, or pay attention to history and Indigenous ingredients," she wrote in one Facebook post. "And then sometimes, after all that research, I decide that the obvious choice is the right one. So for Sweden, we went for Swedish meatballs with boiled herbed potatoes, lingonberries, homemade pickles, and a Nordic slaw."

Travel Tuesdays turned out to be so much fun that she kept the tradition going long after the pandemic subsided. "It was a spontaneous idea that ended up bringing us lots of joy, both as a family and in some of the really great conversations it has sparked with others," Jennifer said. "It turns out to be a great conversation starter—I've connected with strangers all over the world through this topic."

As much as we relish Jennifer's Facebook posts, neither of us has found the time to make Nordic slaw or homemade pickles in our busy everyday lives. Indeed, one of the benefits of travel may be that it creates space in our calendars for novel experiences and enjoyable activities that get crowded out of everyday life. Happily, new research points to a way around this problem. In a series of studies, full-time workers in the US were randomly assigned to experiment with one weekend.[7] Some of them were told, "Treat this weekend like a vacation. That is, to the extent possible, think in ways and behave in ways as though you were on a vacation." Others were told to think and behave the way they would on any ordinary weekend.

Remarkably, even without traveling anywhere, the "vacationers" felt happier during the weekend and were still enjoying a mood boost when they returned to work on Monday. Compared with the people who had an ordinary weekend, they reported spending more time eating and enjoying "intimate relations." They also spent less time working and doing chores around the house. But these differences didn't seem to account for the Monday mood boost. Instead, what really seemed to matter was that treating the weekend like a vacation helped people stay present in the moment, providing a mental reset that left them feeling refreshed by Monday. Compared with ordinary weekenders, vacationers were less likely to say that they "rushed through activities without really being attentive to them" or "found it difficult to pay attention to the 'here and now.'"

So, treating the weekend like a vacation may boost your happiness at almost no cost in terms of carbon. Liz tried this strategy recently, over Mother's Day weekend. After announcing her Mother's Day vacation to her husband and son, she booked a facial at a local spa and carved out part of Saturday to go mountain biking in the nearby forest. But by Sunday, her cluttered desk begged to be cleaned and she found herself in front of her computer, answering email rather than focusing on the present moment.

To escape the siren song of household chores and familiar weekend routines, JZ and her wife, Kirsten, have turned the weekend into a vacation several times a year by booking a hotel room in Vancouver. Each time, they choose a different neighborhood, which puts them into the tourist mindset. They visit local markets and historical sites and check out the neighborhood's best restaurants. These weekends have left JZ with deep knowledge of Vancouver and a greater sense of belonging and attachment to her adopted hometown.

At check-in, JZ and Kirsten are often asked where they're from. When they respond, "Oh, twelve blocks away!" the hotel staff members often laugh with surprise and start looking for a free room upgrade to a higher floor. JZ especially loves staying in hotel towers that offer an aerial view of her own condo, giving her a taste of what astronauts experience when they look back on Earth from space. This experience of seeing a familiar place from above is known as the "overview effect," and astronauts—as well as ordinary people in VR headsets—report feeling a shift in awareness accompanied by a sense of interconnection and awe.[8] In a famous essay titled "Why We Travel," Pico Iyer writes, "We travel, initially, to lose ourselves; and we travel, next, to find ourselves."[9] JZ has been surprised to discover that traveling just twelve blocks can help her do both.

Limiting our world travel may also make us better at savoring simple but pleasant tourist attractions. To explore this idea, Liz and her student Jordi Quoidbach conducted a field experiment at Boston's Old North Church.[10] Liz grew up in Boston, but her family never got around to visiting the Old North Church, which is the fourteenth stop on Boston's historic Freedom Trail. The church is charming, but not exactly spectacular. One visitor, who had traveled everywhere from New Zealand to the Mediterranean and the Baltic Sea, commented that he was "not too impressed with the rather plain interior." He added, "After visiting churches all over the world, this venue was rather disappointing."

It's easy to see how the Old North Church might pale in comparison to Sacré-Coeur or Westminster Abbey. But Liz and Jordi wondered if merely *feeling* like a globetrotter might impair people's capacity to savor simple tourist attractions. So, they gave tourists a travel quiz on their way into the Old North Church. Liz and Jordi carefully rigged the quiz so that it left some people feeling like they were very well traveled and others feeling like they hardly ever got to go anywhere. Then, they measured how much time these visitors spent exploring the Old North Church. The people who felt well traveled rushed in and out of the church. But those who felt like homebodies spent almost 50 percent more time enjoying this historic landmark.

The limits on travel imposed by the pandemic helped Brendan McCabe, a photographer based in Washington, D.C., to savor simple tourism experiences more.[11] After canceling other trips, his family was only able to visit nearby Sandbridge Beach, in southeastern Virginia. "There, amid all the chaos and noise that was 2020, I found myself at peace," he wrote. "I concentrated on small moments, like finding sand crabs with my kids, watching dolphins at dawn, and surfing or stand-up paddleboarding in the ocean. Suddenly, these familiar activities had greater value."

So, exploring close to home can help us enjoy low-carbon tourism experiences that we might easily overlook. And restricting our travel—even temporarily—might help to restore our capacity to savor simple pleasures.

Cutting Carbon at Thirty Thousand Feet

In one of our favorite comedic rants, Chris Rock says, "Remember it used to be fun to fly? You could have, like, a twelve o'clock flight, leave your house at eleven thirty . . . and make it." But things have changed. "They got all this security. They take your shoes. They take your shampoo. When did shampoo become so dangerous? They take your shampoo, you get through security, and they sell shampoo at the gift shop. Sometimes, they're trying to sell you your own shampoo back."[12] The hassles of flying are compounded by its dizzying carbon costs. Indeed, a single round-trip flight from Portland to Paris burns nearly as much carbon as the average person living in Kenya burns in a year. Cutting back on flights is an obvious sweet spot for reducing both stress and carbon. But more than half of Americans flew during 2024, most of them for personal reasons rather than work.[13] In fact, neither of us has totally given up flying—but we try to follow a few key principles when we fly.

Carry-on Joy

By nature, Liz is not a light packer. Years ago, when she flew to Berlin to surprise a friend, she packed a suitcase that was large enough for her to fit inside it (indeed, after unpacking, she popped out of the suitcase to greet her astonished friend). But times have changed. When her giant checked bag got lost on a trip to the Outer Banks of North Carolina—and she spent much of her beach week stuck on the phone with the airline—she swore to avoid checking luggage whenever possible. This strategy allows her to begin her vacation as soon as she lands, breezing past her fellow passengers standing anxiously by the baggage carousel (as columnist Erma Bombeck quipped, "Did you ever notice that the first piece of luggage on the carousel never belongs to anyone?").[14]

When it comes to saving carbon, luggage matters. It turns out that packing a typical checked bag is equivalent to bringing an extra six-year-old child along with you (though, admittedly, the bag is less likely to demand snacks).

Liz has learned to pack a light carry-on by harnessing the capsule wardrobe concept discussed in chapter 3. On a recent trip to France, she was surprised to discover that one black dress could be lightly accessorized to work for a beach stroll in a surfside village or a night out in Paris. Her new favorite carry-on bag was made by the Canadian-Norwegian designer Adrian Solgaard, who told us that the inspiration for the suitcase came in part from living with ADHD. He finds small forms of friction—like unpacking a bag—extremely grating, so he designed a carry-on suitcase that turns into a traveling closet. His goal is to give people an extra twenty minutes of vacation time by largely eliminating the pointless exercise of putting clothes away in hotel drawers.

Of course, even the most devout carry-on-only travelers may find themselves checking bags when they fly with young children. Babies and toddlers seem to require a cornucopia of supplies, from diapers and sippy cups to strollers and car seats. Before having kids, Kyla Hunter, the Canadian optometrist who coined the term "Toonie Party" featured in chapter 3, was fanatical about carry-on travel. "My husband and I would battle for who could pack the lightest, which sometimes resulted in him forgetting lots of things," Kyla told us. "He'd be like, 'Yeah, I packed the lightest!' And I'm like, 'Yeah, well, you brought one shirt with you. So that doesn't count.'"

When their older daughter turned two and the younger one was just a baby, they packed for their first big family trip to Asia—and decided to stick with carry-on only. What are you going to do about diapers?" she recalls her baffled friends asking. She told them, "We're going to buy them when we get there. The whole world has diapers. We don't have to bring four weeks' worth of diapers from Canada."

Not only that, but rental companies have popped up in vacation destinations to offer families everything they need for an easy trip with babies and toddlers. One such company, Maui Baby Rentals, offers everything from bouncy chairs and exersaucers to cribs and car seats, delivered free right to the airport or hotel (despite their name, they do not actually rent babies).

Once Kyla's daughters were out of diapers, the family embarked on a yearlong trip around the world—with only carry-on luggage. The kids, aged five and six, carried their own clothing in their backpacks. "A lot of people get caught up in bringing all these things to entertain their kids," she said. "If you get them in the habit of needing these things to be entertained, then they are going to need them to be entertained." Because they weren't loaded down with toys and the other detritus of family life, they were able to get around more seamlessly. "It's a lot easier to take public transit because we've just got everything on our backs," she said. So, sticking to a light carry-on bag can not only reduce your carbon footprint when you fly, but help you choose more sustainable forms of travel once you're on the ground.

Choose the Exit Row

In a rant about the misery of flying economy class, YouTube star Josiah Schneider complained, "There's literally no leg room, like, my chair is touching the one in front of it. . . . How am I supposed to sit in here for five hours?"[15] If you find yourself crammed into a tiny economy class seat next to a passive-aggressive row-mate slow-fighting you for the armrest, you can at least console yourself that you're minimizing your carbon footprint. Still, it's hard not to look enviously at business class—which in Josiah's eyes "comes with a twin-size bed, a flat-screen TV, Wi-Fi, a personal masseuse, your own private bathroom, and a freshly cooked custom meal by a professional chef . . . [for] five thousand dollars." Even without the personal masseuse, a standard business class seat will double or triple your personal carbon cost (not to mention the hefty financial cost). Every airplane has a sweet spot, though: the exit row. On the Boeing 737-800, the distance between seats is a mere thirty-one inches in economy class (Josiah was not wrong!), compared with thirty-eight inches in business class.[16] But the exit row comes in at thirty-seven inches, nearly matching business class. Because an escape route is a necessary safety feature, we think of the exit row as a guilt-free choice for finding some comfort at thirty thousand feet.

Ditch Layovers

While planning a summertime vacation to New York City, JZ was faced with a dilemma: She could buy a nonstop flight from Vancouver to NYC or choose a one-stop for half the price. She opted to save money. It was the worst decision ever. The layover was in Atlanta—which anyone who has ever seen a map knows is *not* on the way from Vancouver to New York. And Atlanta was blanketed in thunderstorms, creating a cascade of flight delays. When JZ finally landed in New York City, feeling as though she had just flown to Tokyo—which would've taken about the same amount of time—she swore she would always pony up the cash for direct flights.

Although nonstop flights cost about 20 percent more, on average, they are the frugal choice when it comes to carbon.[17] The most carbon-intensive part of a flight is takeoff, as the plane fights gravity to get into the sky. More important, a direct route minimizes the number of miles you're traveling, particularly compared with circuitous options like JZ's swing through Atlanta. In fact, JZ's tortuous flight to NYC cost almost 50 percent more carbon compared with the direct flight. And the nonstop flight would have gotten her to New York City in time for a fun dinner with friends. Instead, she spent the first evening of her vacation in the Atlanta airport—hours of her life that she will never get back.

The Magic of Bundling

If you have to fly a lot for work, then it's worth considering whether you could turn these utilitarian trips into vacations. For example, when JZ was invited to give a TED Talk on our research in New York City, she extended her trip to see friends, do some sightseeing, and go to a comedy show (and TED covered the pricey direct flight!).[18]

It took Liz longer to learn this lesson. When she was asked to give a talk for a major bank in Indonesia, she decided to spend just over twenty-four hours in the faraway country. When she landed, a representative from the bank met her at the airport and looked askance at the rumpled yoga pants and sweatshirt Liz had worn on the eighteen-hour flight.

"Did you get my message that you should wear a batik for the talk?" the banker asked nervously. Seeing Liz's confusion, she clarified, "You know . . . a batik—a dress." Liz reassured her that she had, in fact, packed a dress and would not be stepping onstage in yoga pants. But she soon learned that batik was a traditional Indonesian fabric. She had not packed any batik, so she spent her brief amount of free time in sunny Indonesia combing through a giant shopping mall, searching for a suitable dress. She found an all-batik store, and a helpful saleswoman pointed out several possibilities, none of which Liz liked. But then Liz spotted a pretty dress and took it to the counter to pay. The saleswoman hesitated, and then said, as politely as possible, "Umm, that's a nightgown."

After nearly delivering a talk in a nightgown, Liz realized that there might be some value in taking a little extra time to get to know the cultures she visited for work. Of course, tacking on vacation time isn't always easy, given the demands of work and family. But taking even a little extra time can go a long way. When Liz was asked to give a talk in Madrid recently, she added on just one extra day, which enabled her to go on a tapas crawl of the city. She indulged in fried pork belly, tasted olive oil that she still thinks about in her quiet moments, and sipped sangria in a cozy bodega, quenching her thirst for European travel.

Flights Are like Ice Cream

In a somewhat devious study, researchers asked a small number of female dieters to taste ice cream, and they surreptitiously measured how much the women ate.[19] Before bringing out the ice cream, the researchers asked some of the women to drink milkshakes. One might assume that after drinking milkshakes, the dieters would minimize their ice cream consumption. But in fact, just the opposite pattern emerged: Starting with a milkshake led the dieters to eat *more* ice cream. Although this was a small study, it illustrates a phenomenon many of us have experienced, which the researchers termed the "what-the-hell effect." Once we indulge a little, it's tempting to throw our personal rules to the wind.

We've found ourselves thinking this way about flying: If we are going to step on a plane, we might as well go across the world. But when it comes to air travel, the distance you fly matters—a lot. If you live in New England and want to trade mud season for a beach vacation, you could fly direct from Boston to Honolulu, at a cost of more than two thousand pounds of carbon. But choosing the pink-sand beaches of Bermuda instead would cut the carbon cost of your trip by about 70 percent.

Compared with long-haul flights, short flights of just a few hours carry surprisingly low carbon price tags. Because planes have become more efficient, the carbon cost of flying—per passenger, per mile—is actually about the same as or even lower than the carbon cost of driving a typical gas car. For example, a three-hour direct flight from Minneapolis to Orlando burns less than nine hundred pounds of carbon per person (round trip), whereas driving a gas car would burn more than twenty-eight hundred pounds. If you pack at least four people into the car, then driving is the more efficient option, but otherwise, flying wins.

So, it's really the long-haul flights—from, say, Vancouver to Madrid—that we most need to minimize. And if you are going to take a carbon-heavy long-haul flight, then it's worth staying for as long as possible, because most of the carbon cost comes from getting there and back. For example, if you live in Minneapolis, it would be much better to spend a month in Europe every four years than to go for a week every summer. Think of long-haul travel like the Olympics—something very special that shouldn't happen too often.

Get off the Plane

Cutting back on flying invites us to consider more enjoyable ways of exploring new places. Cat Jones embraced flight-free travel, and by her twenties, she was hopping on trains, boats, and bikes from her home in London to craft delightful holidays for herself and her family. Cat's friends envied her unique way of getting around, and she insisted that they could do it, too. But, she told us, her friends found the amount of planning involved to be paralyzing. "It was a huge amount of work to research all of those train timetables and ferry timetables," she admitted. "When you're going on multiple trains and multiple ferries, if one bit goes wrong, the knock-on effects can be huge. I'd compile ring binders of printed-out timetables." She enjoyed the challenge—and had time for it.

Things changed when she had kids. "I no longer had the time," she told us. She wished there was a company that would do the planning for her. In the lull of the pandemic, she decided to create one. "Our very first mainstream media coverage was in *The Guardian*," she told us, and she recalled that the lovely article had undertones of "crazy lady sets up travel business in global pandemic."

Her company, Byway, makes it easy for people to create their own flight-free adventures, which, she told us, are "optimized for enjoyment." Rather than trying to get people between places as quickly as possible, Byway's algorithm considers "subjective time." As Cat explained, "Time flies when you're having fun, so in our system, time is shorter if the route is highly enjoyable." For example, a lovely four-hour train journey—featuring a scenic stop, stunning views, and amazing food in the dining car—would get a better subjective time score than a ninety-minute train ride that lacked any special food or scenery. This approach encourages vacationers to slow down. When the company started, the average traveler booked a nine-day trip, but the average soon grew to fourteen days. This slower approach to travel can dramatically cut carbon. While flying from London to Paris burns about 236 pounds of carbon, taking the Eurostar train burns just nine pounds.

By harnessing technology to integrate the timetables that once filled Cat's paper binders, Byway removes the friction of planning flight-free vacations, while offering evocative details that enhance anticipation. For example, an eleven-day journey out of London includes a train trip on the Rhaetian Railway to Switzerland, which "passes across 196 bridges and through 55 tunnels as it snakes its way over the Bernina Pass, 2253 metres [7,392 feet] above sea level. This is one of the most spectacular railway journeys on Earth, so be sure to have your camera at the ready!"[20]

When it comes to maximizing the joy of travel, these tantalizing details matter. In a scientific article titled "Waiting for Merlot," Amit Kumar and his colleagues argue that anticipation is a core component of the pleasure that experiential purchases provide.[21] In one study, they sent thousands of adults multiple iPhone notifications, asking them each time, "Are you currently thinking about a purchase you intend to make (either a material good like a TV or item of clothing, or an experience like a vacation or concert)?"[22] Remarkably, Amit's team found that people spent nearly 20 percent of their waking hours thinking about upcoming purchases—and compared with material purchases, thinking about experiential purchases generated more happiness and excitement (and less impatience).

Of course, it's easier to get excited about taking the Rhaetian Railway to Switzerland than hopping on a typical Amtrak route in North America. After taking Amtrak from Vancouver to Seattle together recently, we swore we would never do it again. The train made numerous unplanned stops, in part for maintenance on the rails, and when we asked a staff member about the arrival time, he responded by telling us that he had never actually seen the train arrive on time. The bathroom sink had a sign that read, "Hand washing only," leading us to wonder what other body parts people had attempted to wash. As the train shook its way into the Seattle station, JZ calculated that a round-trip flight would have cost each of us 243 pounds of carbon, while the train cost 97 pounds each—meaning we saved the equivalent of about three hamburgers each way. The train took five times as long as flying, and the subjective time felt even longer.

A smarter strategy would have been for us to rent an electric vehicle to drive to Seattle. Because the Pacific Northwest uses clean energy, sharing an EV would have burned only forty pounds of carbon total, for the two of us. And for that family driving from Minneapolis to Orlando, renting an EV would burn 710 pounds of carbon in total—less than the carbon cost of a round-trip flight for just one person. Not only that, but renting an EV can provide an opportunity for gas car owners to experience the quiet comfort of an electric car. Cat told us that the limited train network in North America has been a barrier to bringing Byway here—but that EV rentals could help to bridge this gap.

North America also lags behind Europe in offering opportunities for cycling tourism—the lowest-carbon form of transportation. But this is beginning to change. In 2022, Tourisme Montréal launched the Véloroute Gourmande (or gourmet bike route), a 150-mile bike track peppered with culinary attractions. As they make their way from Montreal to the city of Sherbrooke, cyclists can stop at farm-to-table restaurants, wineries, cider houses, and confectionaries.

Suzanne Podhaizer, a chef and aspiring cyclist, took a Greyhound bus to Montreal from her home in Vermont in order to explore the Véloroute Gourmande. "Not only did I get to sample foie gras pâté with massive local blueberries, sip gin scented with sea buckthorn, and spread local cranberry compote on my pancakes," Suzanne recalled, "I also got to test my mettle by pedaling through the bucolic Canadian landscape from which the ingredients came."[23] For those who are more interested in tasting foie gras than testing their mettle, e-bikes are available to rent, so the experience isn't only accessible to spandex-clad weekend warriors. In fact, retired people have flocked to the Véloroute Gourmande, where they can take their time and map out their own unique experience.

While bikes, EVs, and trains all offer low-carbon alternatives to flying, the picture is more complicated when it comes to boats. Generally speaking, it's much better to fly than take a cruise. A couple in need of a romantic getaway could fly from New York City to the Bahamas and stay in a luxury hotel for seven nights at a total carbon cost of less than one ton. But taking a seven-night cruise from New York to the Bahamas would cost them 4.2 tons. As sustainable tourism expert O'Shannon Burns told us, a cruise ship is basically a "floating hotel, burning fossil fuels in the middle of the ocean." While planes just transport people and their luggage, cruise ships carry restaurants, pools, and even go-kart racetracks and planetariums, creating outsize emissions.[24]

The cruise industry is beginning to recognize the need for change. O'Shannon recently got to experience the future of cruising on a voyage with Hurtigruten, Norway's coastal cruise line. Hurtigruten has built the world's first hybrid cruise ships, which run partly on batteries. The ships feature restaurants and hot tubs, but no go-kart racetracks. "It's a Norwegian style of luxury," O'Shannon told us.

The hybrid ships have to stop in multiple ports along the way in order to charge. Their system depends on the cooperation of local communities. Unlike major cruise lines that dump throngs of visitors on overwhelmed cities, Hurtigruten is deeply connected to the fabric of small towns along the Norwegian coast. The ships deliver mail and medical supplies to remote communities, and a percentage of each ship is reserved for locals. So, a kids' soccer team might hop on board your cruise to catch a ride to a tournament in another town. Carly Biggert, who works for Hurtigruten, told us that children sometimes wave Norwegian flags as the ships come into port.

Carly told us, "North Americans like to complain about cabin size, but it's meant to be cozy. It's just meant to be your bedroom." Rather than hanging out in their cabins, travelers are encouraged to spend time in what Hurtigruten calls "living rooms," which feature comfortable seats facing large windows that offer stunning views of the passing scenery. "You need to let go of all your preconceived notions of cruising," Carly tells travelers. "And a lot of the time at the end, they'll say, 'This was a life-changing event for me.'"

Indeed, part of the reason why experiential purchases make people happy is that experiences such as travel contribute to their life stories in a way that material purchases rarely do.[25] Experiences also feel unique, whereas material things are easy to compare. And research shows that this sense of uniqueness helps to insulate people from buyer's remorse, even when experiences don't work out perfectly.[26] O'Shannon told us about hitting bad weather on board her Hurtigruten cruise—but she said this with a smile, explaining that her experience felt richer and more adventurous because of it.

In nearby Sweden, Kimberly Nicholas upped the adventure

quotient even further by purchasing a used sailboat, built in the 1970s. Kim grew up in California, where her family still lives. After moving to Sweden to take a faculty position in sustainability science at Lund University, she longed to visit her family but wanted to avoid high-carbon international flights. So, she and her husband decided they would learn to sail. Their dream is to sail to California, but so far, their biggest trip has been from Sweden to Denmark, about twenty nautical miles. "It's not that far. But it was a big deal for us. That was five weeks after we bought the boat, and we are real beginners," she said. "So, that felt like a big accomplishment."

She's ordered an electric motor for the boat, but for now, the boat has a gas motor. Still, she told us, "Ninety-nine percent of the time, it's zero-carbon because we're using wind energy," and she's only gone through a couple of gallons of gas since buying the boat. Working on the science of climate change can be emotionally exhausting, so, she said, "I'm prioritizing joy in my life: sailing and family and friends and food and sunshine and gardening and the things that make me really happy."

Staying Happy

So far, we've focused on modes of transportation—planes, trains, automobiles, and so on—that account for the lion's share of tourism emissions. But what about accommodations? It turns out that it doesn't matter all that much whether you stay in a quirky Airbnb, a luxury hotel, or a campground. Entirely by chance, JZ recently stayed in a Toronto hotel that bills itself as a "sustainable sanctuary." Instead of the usual plastic room key, JZ was handed a wood chip. There was no single-use anything. To indicate whether she wanted housekeeping, she was given a rock, which said "now" on one side and "not now" on the other. Although the hotel was charming, JZ's back-of-the-napkin calculations suggested that these performative gestures probably didn't save much carbon.

When it comes to hotels, what matters most is whether they use renewable energy. Going beyond wooden room keys, Two Bunch Palms—a wellness resort on the outskirts of Palm Springs—installed a 3.5-acre solar farm that supplies power for the hotel's luxurious rooms. The property sits on the San Andreas Fault, providing naturally heated water that bubbles into the resort's pools and hot tubs. As well as "taking the waters," guests can participate in Reiki meditation, a guided nature walk, or "quantum breathing." The resort's manager, Ankit Sekhri, describes it as "adult summer camp." He told us that 90 percent of guests come from Los Angeles, with many of them making the two-hour drive in EVs, keeping their total travel footprint low.

The luxury of Two Bunch Palms stands in contrast to what might seem like the greenest accommodation of all: camping. Staying in a tent obviously saves electricity, and most campgrounds offer little in the way of carbon-heavy amenities. But camping has a hidden carbon cost. Many campers light fires for hot dogs and s'mores or simply warmth and ambience. And these fires can get out of control. The largest wildfire in Arizona's history was started by two experienced campers who inadvertently left their campfire smoldering after cooking breakfast.[27] This fire alone generated more than eighty million tons of carbon. In the United States, 85 percent of wildfires are caused by humans, including through unattended campfires.[28] So, at least in hot, dry weather, it might be better to choose a luxurious hotel over a tent.

Renting an Airbnb is another sweet spot, especially if you're traveling with a big group of friends. Compared with getting individual hotel rooms, sharing a house tends to be a relatively carbon-light option.[29] Plus, renting a group house can create more opportunities for casual socializing. And Liz's latest research suggests that the more time we make for socializing, the better. Her team analyzed detailed time-use data from more than forty thousand Americans.[30] They found that spending time with others made virtually every activity of the day more enjoyable—even typically solitary activities like reading and thinking. So, alone time may be overrated.

Offsetting Climate Guilt

When JZ booked her recent trip to Toronto, the airline offered her the opportunity to offset the half-ton of carbon she was burning with her flight—for only seventeen dollars. She declined. Carbon offsets seem like an alluring way to buy guilt-free travel. But they are often a sham.

One of our favorite academic papers on this topic is titled,

"Do Carbon Offsets Offset Carbon?"[31] In short, the answer appears to be no. Economist Rafael Calel analyzed the world's largest carbon offset program and found that at least half the offsets were not moving the needle on emissions.

"A lot of different things are called *carbon offsetting*," O'Shannon explained. "And the reality is that there are a lot of junk offsets out there." When Liz first heard about carbon offsets, she imagined giant fans sucking carbon out of the air. And these fans do exist. The technology is called direct air capture, but the problem, at least for now, is that powering the fans burns more carbon than the fans suck out.[32] A lower-tech approach involves planting trees, which also capture carbon. Young trees don't capture much, though, meaning it can take ten years or more for the benefits to emerge.[33] So, planting a tree to save carbon is a little like having a baby to get help around the house. Another approach is to protect existing forests, but it can be hard to know whether you're protecting forests that are actually under threat.

So, like JZ, O'Shannon declines the offsets she's offered when she books flights. "Today, I need to book two trips," she told us. "I'm not going to have the time to investigate how each airline approaches offsetting." Rather than relying on the black box of offsets provided by airlines, rental cars, or travel agencies, O'Shannon takes a more thoughtful—and joyful—approach. "At the end of each year I give myself a gift. I look at all the travel I've done for the year and estimate my emissions. And then I really take the time to find a project that's meaningful to me."

JZ uses a similar strategy. She offset her Toronto trip by

funding clean cookstoves for families in Nigeria, an innovative carbon offset program from the nonprofit Gold Standard.[34] More than 80 percent of families in Nigeria lack access to clean cooking, and trees are cut down to provide cooking fuel, which contributes to indoor air pollution. By providing subsidized cookstoves to families who otherwise could not afford them, this program protects trees that are under direct threat, while also protecting the health of at-risk families. Plus, these efficient, modern cookstoves reduce the burden of fuel collection and cooking, increasing time affluence for Nigerian women.

Because JZ understands the positive impact of her money, she finds joy in offsetting her travel in this way (and we are offsetting this book with the same approach). JZ thinks of shopping for carbon offsets, even with Gold Standard, as being a little like shopping at a thrift store—there's a lot of junk, but there are also some gems, and it's exciting to find them. Like the inventory at a thrift store, the offerings at Gold Standard are always changing, so it's worth spending some time exploring when you're in a treasure-hunting mood. JZ recommends staying away from funding wind farms and reforestation projects—because the benefits can be tough to ascertain—and looking instead for projects like the Nigerian cookstoves, which enable households to change fuel sources.

Alternatively, you could help your *own* household change fuel sources by creating a carbon savings account. If you want to buy a heat pump, solar panels, or a used EV, but can't quite afford it, then creating a designated savings account could help you achieve your goal. Classic research shows that having a dedicated account for a specific purpose helps people save more money.[35] When JZ offsets her travel with Gold Standard, she donates twenty to thirty US dollars per ton of carbon, but if you're putting the money into your own personal carbon savings account, you might consider increasing this amount to fifty dollars or more per ton.

Of course, it's tempting to think that we don't need to offset our travel because seeing the world is inherently transformational. As Xavier Font puts it, there is a popular notion that "when we travel, we have an epiphany because we see a polar bear, and then we come back home, and we are better people." As he launched into a critique of this idea, Xavier began, "Spoiler alert: bullshit." There's no good evidence that travel turns people into more environmentally responsible citizens. But there is very clear evidence that travel can provide an important source of joy and connection. So, rather than giving up travel, or suppressing our feelings of guilt, it's worth confronting those feelings directly and embracing joyful, lower-carbon forms of travel.

CHAPTER 6

Life's Biggest Decisions

John-Robert Rodriguez was raised in South Florida, in what he calls the "suburbs of the suburbs." While he was in college, his family moved to the outskirts of Austin, Texas, and when he found himself unemployed after graduation, he moved in with them. "I had to figure out how to make new social connections in the suburbs of Texas. I felt like everyone was thirty-five and in tech. It was a very, very bleak place for me."

Life revolved around cars. And driving everywhere created what John-Robert calls "casual anger." He explained, "I'm not talking about road rage. I'm talking about frustration." When people are arguing over driving and parking, "there are these micro-moments of tension."

Then he got an email that changed his life. A new car-free community called Culdesac was opening in Tempe, Arizona.

Residents could get free bikes and transit passes, plus discounts on ride-sharing and e-scooters. The community offered a pool and coworking space, as well as monthly barbecues and other events designed to connect residents with their neighbors. In 2023, John-Robert rented a one-bedroom apartment and got on a plane to Arizona.

"Culdesac feels like a nice little village," he told us. "I know most of the people here." When we spoke to John-Robert, he was cat-sitting for his next-door neighbor. He explained that because people see each other all the time, it feels easy and natural to help one another.

John-Robert initially got a job as a teacher, commuting for twenty minutes on the light rail into downtown Tempe. But then he made a career move, taking a job in creative consulting. "I work remotely, which I never wanted to do," he said. But living in Culdesac made remote work tolerable. "I very much like face-to-face connection, and I'm glad I work from home in Culdesac, because otherwise I probably would not be getting any kind of social engagement."

He told us that if he has kids someday, he would want to raise them in a community like Culdesac. As a teacher, he observed that most learning actually happened at home. "I would find it a privilege to expose my kids to this kind of environment," he said. Growing up in a car-free community where everyone looks out for their neighbors would shape "what they see as the future."

In this chapter, we're here to help you think through your

own future. We'll tackle major life choices: where to settle, what kind of career to pursue, whether to have kids—the kinds of questions you hope your extended family doesn't ask you about at Thanksgiving dinner. According to a 2024 global survey, over two thirds of the world's population feel that climate change has affected their big decisions, such as where to live or work.[1] Let's find your sweet spot.

Where to Live

The average American moves eleven times.[2] Making a move means overcoming a variety of barriers, including psychological ones. Indeed, even after seeing their homes decimated by climate-related disasters, people often return to the same vulnerable communities, placing themselves in the path of future devastation. And sociologists have discovered that a major reason underlying this seemingly irrational choice is that people simply can't envision where else they would live.[3] So, even if you're not ready to make a move right now, it's worth taking a few minutes to imagine what life could be like somewhere else.

John Jenkins grew up surfing in Southern California, but before having children, he and his wife made a big move, to Duluth, Minnesota. Reflecting on the reasons for their decision, he says, "It wasn't just one thing, but climate was a big one. It's safer here." The city is known as "climate-proof Duluth" because its cool temperatures protect it from the searing heat and forest fires that are becoming increasingly common elsewhere. And when it comes to happiness, Minnesota ranks fifth in life satisfaction out of all fifty states.[4]

Of course, the Midwest isn't for everyone. But there are places across North America—and around the world—that are good bets for finding happiness on a changing planet. In the pages that follow, we propose a simple framework for evaluating places to live based on four key factors.

Heat

It looks like there might be a perfect temperature for human happiness: 65 degrees Fahrenheit (18 degrees Celsius). If it's 65 degrees outside, people don't need to heat or cool their homes to feel comfortable indoors. And when researchers examined life satisfaction levels in 79 countries around the world, they found that the less often temperatures deviated from 65 degrees, the more satisfied people felt with their lives.[5] This relationship held up even when the researchers controlled for a smorgasbord of other variables, from the nation's GDP to its level of freedom.

While extreme levels of both heat and cold can take a toll, people are pretty good at adapting to frigid temperatures. In contrast, peak monthly temperature emerged as the strongest climate-related predictor of diminished life satisfaction across nearly forty countries, with those in the hottest countries faring the worst.[6] For thousands of years, human beings have huddled in a surprisingly narrow band of the planet, where average annual temperatures hover on the cool side of sixty-five, falling

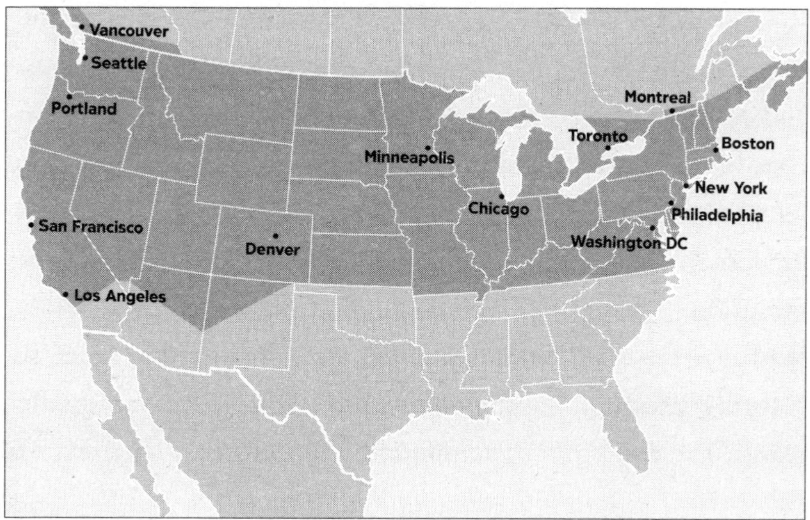

Suitable regions for human inhabitation by 2070, based on projected climate change. Adapted from Xu et al. (2020)[8]

somewhere in the mid to high fifties. Because this pattern is so consistent across history, scientists argue that this temperature band may represent the "human climate niche," where our species is naturally able to thrive.[7] And they anticipate that this human climate niche may shift more over the next fifty years than it has in the preceding six millennia. If current trends continue, many of the southern US states will slip outside of the human climate niche by 2070 (see the map above).

The narrow band shown on the map may make you feel like we're living on an increasingly uninhabitable planet. But it's important to remember that most of the earth has always been uninhabitable (or at least unpleasant to inhabit). We find it reassuring to know that for thousands of years, humans have made do with a relatively slim band of the planet.

And there is some elasticity in this band. By recognizing that climate change is happening now, communities can take concrete steps to enhance resilience—including reducing concrete. Paved surfaces and concrete buildings trap heat and raise temperatures in cities, creating "urban heat islands." In Medellín, Colombia, concern over rising temperatures—along with air pollution—spurred the city to create "green corridors," leafy, shaded streets that connected parks and other natural areas. By planting nearly a million trees and a cornucopia of smaller plants, the city reduced temperatures by close to four degrees Fahrenheit.[9]

We know that cooler temperatures are good for our happiness, but when people consider moving, they often fail to take summer heat into consideration, focusing instead on winter weather. According to Harvard economist Edward Glaeser, "No variable better predicts metropolitan-area growth over the last 120 years than January temperature."[10] On chilly winter days in Vancouver, we confess to fantasizing about lying by a pool in Palm Springs, California. But in a paper titled "Does Living in California Make People Happy?" researchers showed that people overestimate the emotional benefits of moving to the state.[11] In fact, people living in the Midwest are just as happy.

So, if a warm climate doesn't deliver happiness, what does? People are consistently happier living in places where they spend less than 30 percent of their income on housing.[12] And unemployment ranks among the most potent predictors of unhappiness.[13] You'll find cheap rent—among the lowest in the country—in Green Bay, Wisconsin, and the nation's lowest unemployment rate in Rapid City, South Dakota. While these places may not seem as tantalizing as moving to a beach-side community, taking the road less traveled may be a better route to long-term happiness.

Fires and Floods: The F-words of Climate change

There is nothing joyful about fires and floods. But careful choices about where to live can reduce our chances of being impacted by these disasters.

The emotional ripple effects of major fires can extend as far as the smoke blows. Wildfire smoke pollutes the air with tiny particles that easily seep into our lungs. Around the world, people report lower life satisfaction in countries where they breathe in more of these particles—which appear to take a bigger toll on happiness than other forms of air pollution.[14] Breathing in these tiny particles makes people feel less physically healthy, partially explaining their lower levels of happiness.[15]

In the summer of 2023, Canada was engulfed in record-breaking wildfires, and wind blew the smoke across the eastern United States, blanketing the Statue of Liberty in an orange haze. Despite these vivid images, the East Coast is still the best bet for avoiding smoke—and projections suggest it will more or less stay this way over the coming decades.[16]

When it comes to flooding, there are two big sources of risk: Major storms cause overflowing lakes and rivers, and melting ice caps lead to rising sea levels. Not only that, but warmer air carries more moisture, making extreme downpours more likely. In

April 2023, South Florida was hit with nearly twenty-six inches of rain in just one day. Fort Lauderdale suffered the most devastating damage, with people and pets trapped inside their flooded homes. The coastal city sits at sea level, and its beautiful rivers, canals, and beaches make it highly vulnerable to flooding. Over time, sea levels are expected to rise at least one foot, and more major cities, including Amsterdam and Bangkok, will be completely flooded by 2050.[17]

This sounds dire, but the good news is that flooding is relatively predictable, so it's possible to make choices about where to live that will reduce your risk of encountering floods. Moving far away from oceans, rivers, or lakes is an obvious way to reduce flood risks. But research suggests that people experience better moods when they are close to water (or what scientists call "blue space").[18] And getting even a few feet above sea level dramatically reduces the risk of flooding. Liz lives just three blocks from the beach, but because these blocks slant gently upward from the sea, flooding is unlikely to pose a major problem in this century. So, before you move anywhere (especially a coastal city like Fort Lauderdale!), it is worth taking a moment to check out an interactive flood map by going to happyclimate.org.

Of course, geography isn't destiny. Creating more green space can reduce the risk of flooding. Traditionally, cities have relied on concrete embankments and drainage pipes to manage flooding, an approach known as "pave, pipe, and pump."[19] But as a doctoral student at Harvard, landscape architect Kongjian Yu, who hails from the same province in China as JZ, proposed a radically different solution. He envisioned "sponge cities," in which pavement would be replaced by ponds, gardens, and wetlands, which absorb water and return it to the ground, facilitating the natural water cycle.[20] As Yu put it, this approach is like "doing tai chi with water," channeling its natural energy rather than fighting it. And his idea caught on. By 2024, more than seventy cities in China—and dozens of cities around the world—had implemented the sponge city approach. In doing so, these cities have not only increased resilience to flooding in the face of extreme storms; they have created more of the green and blue spaces that are linked to enhanced happiness on an average Tuesday.[21]

Sense of Community

In 1995, Chicago experienced its deadliest heat wave ever. But two adjacent neighborhoods on Chicago's South Side, Englewood and Auburn Gresham, fared very differently from each other. When the heat wave struck, both areas were struggling with similarly high levels of poverty and unemployment. Englewood was one of the most dangerous places to be during the heat wave—but Auburn Gresham turned out to be among the safest, with a lower death rate than more affluent neighborhoods.[22]

Why? While Englewood had experienced a declining population and a loss of social cohesion, Auburn Gresham was a tight-knit community, where people knew their neighbors and were active in church and block clubs. "During the heat wave, we were doing wellness checks, asking neighbors to knock on each other's doors," said Betty Swanson, a long-time resident of Auburn Gresham. "The presidents of our block clubs usually know who's alone, who's aging, who's sick. It's what we always do when it's very hot or very cold here."[23]

Across Chicago, people who participated in churches, clubs, or other social groups were significantly less likely to die in the heat wave.[24] In fact, this form of social connection mattered as much as whether people had a working air conditioner in their home.

Strong social connections can also speed up recovery in the wake of natural disasters. After tornadoes swept across Indiana, researchers surveyed nearly three hundred households, asking how long it had taken them to completely recover from the damage.[25] People who were part of close-knit social networks recovered faster. And those who were able to get help from their nearby neighbors bounced back the fastest. Living in a place where you are connected to your neighbors may be one of the best ways to climate-proof yourself.

And when researchers compared the average levels of life satisfaction in more than twelve hundred Canadian neighborhoods, they found that the happiest neighborhoods were those where people felt a strong sense of community.[26] On average, people living in small towns reported feeling happier and more connected to their communities than those living in big cities. More broadly, across North America, Europe, and other parts of the world, people in urban areas report lower life satisfaction—despite the fact that cities offer more abundant access to high-paying jobs, social events, and cultural experiences.

This pattern, which is known as the *urban desirability para-dox*, poses a problem for tackling climate change.[27] In high-income countries, city dwellers have smaller carbon footprints, partly because they tend to drive less, use less energy, and live in smaller homes than their rural counterparts.[28] So, the ultimate sweet spot lies in finding an urban neighborhood with a strong sense of community, like the one John-Robert Rodriguez discovered in Tempe, Arizona.

Low-Carbon Living

It's much easier to live a low-carbon lifestyle in some places than others—without sacrificing your happiness. In thinking about where to live, one of the most important factors to consider is the carbon intensity of the electricity you'll find there. And US states vary dramatically on this dimension. The key metric (bear with us here) is the pounds of carbon emitted per kilowatt-hour of electricity. Within the US, you'll find the lowest carbon levels in Vermont because this state uses 99.6 percent renewable energy, consisting mostly of hydroelectric power from Canada (you're welcome, Vermont!).[29] Other states in the top ten include South Dakota, California, and New Jersey, while the worst states are West Virginia, Wyoming, and Kentucky (go to happyclimate.org to see a ranking of all fifty states).

To understand how much of a difference this makes, consider the amount of carbon emitted by using a single portable AC unit in your living room for seven days. In Vermont, you would emit eight pounds of carbon—the weight of a newborn baby—while in nearby Maine, you'd emit 283 pounds, more than the average weight of an NFL player. And in Wyoming, the same air conditioner would emit 1078 pounds, akin to a full-grown horse. So, if you're concerned about the climate, you don't have to suffer through summer without AC if you choose to live somewhere with low-carbon energy.

Where you live also profoundly shapes how you get around. As discussed in chapter 4, biking is one of the most pleasurable and lowest-carbon forms of transportation, and it's much more practical in places that offer safe, comfortable bike routes. Among large US cities, Minneapolis, Seattle, and San Francisco top the list for bikeability—but the highest scores of all are to be found in small towns such as Provincetown, Massachusetts, and Harbor Springs, Michigan.

Compared with biking, riding public transit isn't such a surefire route to happiness. But in a 2024 poll, more than 80 percent of residents in both New York City and Chicago said that it was easy to get around their cities by transit (and people love easy things!).[30] These cities—along with San Francisco, Boston, and Washington, D.C.—also scored high on an objective indicator of how easy it is to access transit.

In most parts of the country, people are still stuck with driving, but there's lots of variability in commuting time and congestion. It takes almost twice as long to drive in Baltimore as to drive the same distance in Detroit.[31] And if you own an EV or hope to buy one someday, it's helpful to know whether you're moving to an oasis of charging stations or a desert. Not surprisingly, Vermont, California, and Massachusetts lead the country in charging stations per resident.[32] But there are big gaps between seemingly similar cities: for example, Kansas City, Missouri, offers four times as many chargers per resident as Milwaukee, Wisconsin.

By investing in clean energy, transit, sidewalks, bike lanes, and EV chargers, some communities are making it easier for residents to live happier, lower-carbon lives. And choosing to move to one of these communities sends a powerful message to governments and city planners (at happyclimate.org, you can see current ratings of walkability, bikeability, and transit quality for more than a hundred North American cities).

Moving Beyond Climate-Proof Duluth

Applying the framework we've described, the ideal place to move to would offer moderate temperatures, a low risk of fires and floods, a strong sense of community, and climate-friendly policies. And of course, it needs to be affordable and have room for new residents. So, where is this magical place?

The truth is, no place is perfect—even so-called "climate-proof Duluth." For one thing, Duluth's frigid, snowy winters aren't for everybody. "It's basically that barren ice planet from Star Wars," said Michael Kosta, in a segment for *The Daily Show* on this climate refuge. And he asked the city's chief sustainability officer, "Do you think those big UN climate change summits would be more effective if people knew the alternative was having to move to Duluth?"

So, rather than searching for the *perfect* place to live, it may be wiser to consider the trade-offs you're willing to accept—and how far you're willing to go. Natalie Sageloly grew up in northern Canada and didn't dip her toe in the ocean until she was twenty-two years old. In her midtwenties, she moved to Toronto and pursued a career in fashion, which she describes as a *"Devil Wears Prada* situation." But after spending two weeks on vacation in Costa Rica, she decided to uproot her life and move to the surf town of Nosara, on the country's west coast. She told us she had "zero game plan. I didn't want to have a game plan. That's kind of how I roll." She lived in a tin house, worked as a surf instructor, and eventually started her own small business in the tourism industry.

Despite having zero game plan, Natalie stumbled into a haven of happiness and low-carbon living. The country went all in on sustainability, and 95 percent of its energy now comes from renewable sources, allowing residents to live low-carbon lifestyles with minimal sacrifice.[33] While Costa Rica has gotten substantially richer over the past decade, its carbon emissions have remained almost flat.[34]

And residents of Costa Rica report some of the highest levels of positive emotion in the world. From 2018 to 2020, the Gallup organization surveyed people in 147 countries, asking them to report whether they laughed, smiled, and enjoyed themselves the day before. Costa Rica ranked sixth in the world.[35] People there reported experiencing happier days than in Canada (ranked twenty-sixth), the United States (thirtieth), and the UK (forty-sixth).

But does moving to a happier country actually make people happier? The answer appears to be yes. After people immigrate, their happiness ratings correspond more closely to the average happiness levels in their new country, rather than to the average happiness levels back in their home country. And immigrants get a bigger boost from moving to happier countries. For example, one study found that immigrants who move to Canada end up happier than immigrants from the same country who move to the UK.[36]

While we're bragging about Canada, it's worth noting that both Quebec and our home province of British Columbia have more than 97 percent renewable energy. Plus, as the human climate niche moves northward, Canada is looking better and better and may be a particularly appealing alternative for Americans who care about climate change. After Donald Trump won the 2016 US presidential election, the Canadian immigration website got so much traffic that the whole site crashed.

Still, Canada lags behind Costa Rica in joyfulness. Why? Part of the answer seems to lie in the culture of Costa Rica, which prioritizes close relationships between family and friends. Natalie told us, "In our town, it is so easy to make quality friendships and have community—true community. I've never found another place in the world where instantaneously everyone welcomes you with open arms." Nosara is scorching hot in the middle of the day, but as sunset approaches and the temperature begins to drop, folks congregate at the beach, enabling easy, spontaneous meetups. There's no need to plan playdates for the children.

This strong sense of community helps to make the town more resilient in the face of climate challenges. The town is vulnerable to flooding, whenever heavy rainfalls cause the river to overflow. "But again," Natalie told us, "because of our amazing community, everyone joins together. They bring people new mattresses or even help them rebuild their homes."

People have time to help each other and to prioritize social relationships because the pace of life is slower. According to Natalie, "When expats move to Costa Rica, most of them say they are moving here to slow down." But once they settle in, they discover that slowing down doesn't just mean chilling at the beach—it also means waiting around at the bank. "You have to be prepared with snacks and a book. By the time you actually get to the front of the line, the teller will put up a 'closed' sign because he has to go to lunch. It's frustrating—but it's the price you have to pay to live in paradise."

And moving to paradise has gotten more practical. In 2022, Costa Rica introduced a "digital nomad visa," which allows people who are self-employed or who work remotely to move to Costa Rica relatively easily.[37] Still, for most people, decisions about where to live are deeply intertwined with decisions about what kind of career to pursue.

Choosing a Career

Etelle Higonnet is a French knight. But she didn't match our image of a mounted man-at-arms. When she spoke to us over

Zoom, she had just put her baby to bed and told us, "I look like my hair was styled by a one-and-a-half-year-old. I've probably got yogurt on me somewhere. It's fine. The yogurt is fine."

After graduating from Yale Law School, Etelle spent twelve years working on human rights. "I worked a lot in war zones and post-conflict areas. It was a bit grim," she said. "After twelve and a half years, I was smoking half a pack a day, my hair started falling out, and I thought I needed more work-life balance. I wanted to work on something cheerful . . . like climate change!" She went to work for Greenpeace in Southeast Asia. "I loved it and learned so much," she told us.

For good reason, a large organization like Greenpeace was reluctant to send its employees to certain dangerous hot spots where, as Etelle put it, "you could end up in jail for a long time with no recourse." But she and other former Greenpeace employees thought work needed to be done in these places, so they founded a nimble organization called Mighty Earth. They sued companies that were causing deforestation—and won. "I had to go after the biggest companies, toe-to-toe with the biggest rubber, biggest cattle, and biggest cocoa companies," Etelle said. Her work on deforestation was transformative, and she earned the Chevalier de l'Ordre National du Mérite—also known as knighthood.

Still, reflecting on one of her signature achievements, she told us, "It's obviously not perfect. It didn't go from F to A. I would say it went from an F to a C minus. But an F to a C minus is great. That's a big change."

This perspective has helped her stay optimistic in the

daunting fight against climate change. Etelle says, "I'm a huge believer in joy. Despair is the worst. If you sit there and let yourself feel existential angst and despair about climate, you would never do anything. The world is a beautiful place made to have fun in. There's so much we can do. We have so much beautiful, fabulous, kick-ass power."

Working for a nonprofit like Greenpeace or Mighty Earth isn't the only way to exercise that beautiful, fabulous, kick-ass power. Katie Kross, a sustainability educator at Duke University, told us, "Students always come to me and ask, 'What's the *best* work to do, if I want to have the biggest impact on climate?' In my opinion, we need everyone. We need engineers. We need policymakers. We need public health experts. We need marketers. We need investors, venture capitalists, and entrepreneurs. We need everyone working on solutions to the climate crisis in every discipline, so there isn't one best place to make a difference."

And this means there's a lot of room to choose a job that not only makes a difference but also makes you happy. So, what factors matter most for happiness at work? To find out, researchers examined job satisfaction ratings provided by diverse workers across thirty-seven different countries.[38] These workers provided a ton of information about their jobs—everything from how much they got paid and how many hours they worked to whether they experienced difficulty, stress, and danger on the job.

Not surprisingly, the results revealed that money matters—people were happier with higher-paying jobs. But pay was only the third most important factor (see figure). The single most important predictor of job satisfaction was the quality of relationships people found at work. And having an interesting job also mattered more than having a high-paying one.

If you care about climate change, devoting your career to

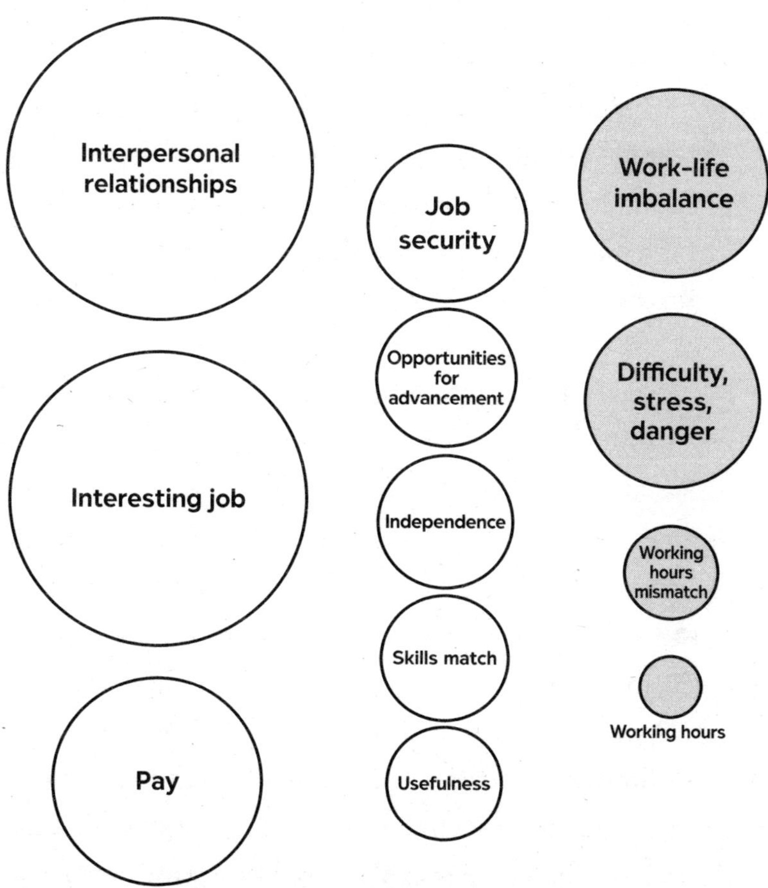

The size of each circle represents the importance of a workplace factor for job satisfaction. The gray circles are associated with lower job satisfaction. Adapted from Krekel et al. (2019).[39]

this issue might seem inherently interesting. As the North American director of the climate nonprofit 350.org, Tamara Toles O'Laughlin worked to bring Greta Thunberg to New York City for 2019's massive climate strike. But, Tamara explained, her job involved "all the unsexy stuff." She told us, "There were, like, a million people running through Foley Square, and my team and I were like, 'Oh, there are not enough toilet paper rolls!' Because you can't have a revolution without toilet paper. It'll end in a half hour if the revolution doesn't have enough toilet paper."

Although working on the logistics of toilet paper doesn't seem very interesting, Tamara sees it differently. Even as a kid, she was fascinated by the underlying infrastructure that made everything work. When other children drank from the water fountain, she wanted to know about the pipes that lay behind it.

Her skill set was a good match with what the job required, and this turns out to be another factor that predicts job satisfaction. Plus, she knew that she was doing useful work, which is also key to job satisfaction (although not as important as whether the job itself is interesting).

But there was a problem. Even though her organization offered generous benefits, including thirty days off per year, she told us, "Nobody was taking time off." As a leader, she tried to fix this. "I would try to figure out all these ways to get people to take time off. I tried modeling it. I tried talking about it."

Eventually, she figured out the root of the problem: "People were afraid that they were going to be taking a rest while other people were working. They would say, 'I can't take days off because the community that I work with never takes any days off.' I was like, 'Wait a minute, so you have the best benefits that I've ever seen. Not enough money, but the benefits are there, and you won't take it because you feel like you would be disrespectful to the people you're trying to form a relationship with?'" Even as Tamara and her colleagues worked to promote sustainability, their own lifestyle wasn't sustainable.

The key factor isn't the sheer number of hours that people work. In fact, in a global study, the number of hours people reported working was essentially unrelated to their job satisfaction (after controlling for pay and other variables).[40] However, the *mismatch* between how much people wanted to work and how much they were actually working did drag down job satisfaction. In particular, people who wished they were working fewer hours felt less satisfied with their jobs—but only a little less. What mattered much more was their feeling of work-life imbalance. When people felt that their work interfered with family life or they had trouble taking time off on short notice, their job satisfaction took a hit. In fact, work-life imbalance mattered about as much as experiencing difficulty, stress, and danger on the job.

So, an important challenge lies in finding a job in sustainability that is, in itself, sustainable. To maximize job satisfaction, your job should be not only useful but also interesting and a good match with your own skill set. It should pay well, but not confront you with constant stress, difficulty, or danger—or suck up so much of your time that you can't do other things that matter to you. You're also likely to be happier with a job that offers opportunities for advancement, some independence, and job security. And working with people you like and respect seems to matter most of all.

Finding a job that offers *all* of these features may be a tall order, but we think one promising sweet spot lies in working for the government, particularly at the state or local level. A study with more than thirty thousand people across twenty-three countries found that folks who worked in the public sector reported elevated life satisfaction.[41] In a large survey within the United States, state and local government employees said they were attracted to their job because of the high levels of job security and work-life balance it offered.[42] And working in state or local government can give you the opportunity for direct input on climate policies that matter in your community, from installing EV chargers and bike lanes to promoting solar panels and green corridors. That said, within the private sector, there are oodles of opportunities to make a difference on climate change while pursuing a career you find enjoyable.

To help her students make sense of these opportunities, Katie Kross developed a simple career matrix, which we've adapted.[43] As the following figure shows, you could consider taking a traditional role or a climate-oriented role, within either a traditional or a climate-oriented organization. You can potentially make a big difference in any of these quadrants, although your day-to-day might feel quite different in each of them.

Taking a climate-oriented role in a traditional organization often entails working on the sustainability team of a big multinational corporation—what Katie calls "the belly of the beast."

Career matrix with example jobs and organizations. Adapted from Kross (2017).[44]

She told us, "I have had some students go do that work and come back to me a few years later and say, 'I'm done. I cannot move the needle on this. I feel like I'm an island. I am not getting enough support. The challenge of turning this supertanker is too big.' On the flip side, I have had other students do the same job who come back to me and say, 'I love it. I love the challenge of trying to move such a big corporation. I love the work that I do to educate my colleagues, our supply chain partners, and our customers.'" One former student of Katie's told her, "I love the battle."

Michiko Namazu, who was a student in JZ's lab, thrives on this battlefield as a sustainability scientist at Uber. Michiko's team created an alternative routing algorithm to help drivers identify shorter routes that would save gas.[45] When they tested the new algorithm against the standard one, they saw that drivers consumed 0.65 percent less fuel. Okay, so less than 1 percent doesn't sound like much. But because of Uber's massive scale, this tweak to the algorithm has already saved more than one million gallons of gas (or about ten thousand tons of carbon). Based on Michiko's evidence, Uber implemented the algorithm across the United States and Europe and plans to expand it to seventy countries. So, Michiko might've saved more carbon than any of JZ's other students, all with this seemingly tiny change.

Whereas Michiko works on the sustainability team of a traditional company, Michelle Armstrong found joy on the opposite side of the matrix, as chief product officer of Arc'teryx, a sustainability-oriented outdoor clothing company. Michelle told us that she grew up "in the middle of the forest." Her mother, who hailed from the Cree First Nation, sewed all her clothing. As a child, Michelle said, "I always wanted something store-bought. But I didn't realize how much knowledge I was gaining about product development—and how passionate I was about it." She learned to abhor waste and overproduction.

She put these values into action by pioneering Arc'teryx's ReCut strategy, which involves turning wasted textiles into beloved products. When a junior member of her team traveled to visit YKK—a Chinese company that makes most of the world's zippers—he spotted "barrels of zippers, in random colors." He learned that they were leftovers from two years of Arc'teryx's orders. He sent photos of all this waste back to Michelle, and her team created a jacket with zippers in these random colors. A gray jacket might come with a teal zipper. "We numbered the jackets, so if we could only make fifty based on the leftover materials, there would be a number inside, between one and fifty. So, when people bought them, they knew they were getting something unique. And I think that drove the value up." The resale market went crazy. Taking this a step further, Michelle's team gathered all the excess materials from their jackets and combined them into ReCut jackets. "We might build a red jacket with a blue zipper, a blue pocket, and a purple band, and it would sell out in minutes."

Although a dedicated team of sustainability experts reported to Michelle, she told us that these employees sometimes complained that they spent all their time reading, in their mission to keep the company on top of the latest sustainability research. Meanwhile, across the company, people with more traditional roles got to take tangible action. Arc'teryx's office buildings were dotted with coffee stations that included oat milk, almond milk, and regular milk, but the receptionist noticed that in some buildings, the regular milk was getting dumped at the end of the day. In the design building, "Pretty much everyone drank oat milk. So, she stopped sending the other milks," Michelle said. "There was still a spot where you could find regular milk. You just couldn't find it at every location." And this small change significantly reduced day-to-day waste, embodying the company's mission.

While there are lots of traditional roles in sustainability-oriented organizations, most people hold traditional roles in traditional organizations. But, you may have heard the saying "Every job is a climate job." In a survey of more than seven thousand private-sector workers across ten countries, 83 percent said they were ready and willing to take climate action in the context of their job, and 70 percent said doing so was important to their motivation and personal well-being.[46] With some ingenuity, it may be possible for many people to reshape their current jobs to make a difference on climate change—without switching to a whole new career.

After spending more than a decade training to be a cancer surgeon, Andrea MacNeill wasn't about to change career paths, but she carved out a new niche as an "eco-surgeon." Andrea grew up in a very small town in the Canadian province of New Brunswick—the province that Liz always forgets about when quizzed on Canada's geography. The town has only gotten smaller since her childhood, although Andrea joked that the census takers just think the population in this rural hunting town is shrinking "because they're not counting the people wearing camo." Her upbringing involved "conservation by necessity. I think the low socioeconomic background just forces a conservation mindset because you don't have the luxury of excess." From an academic perspective, she told us, it was "not the most privileged, enriching environment. But it was a real-world education. And while I may not have read the classics, I can still tell you how to make maple syrup in both French and English."

After earning a scholarship and getting her undergraduate degree, Andrea went to med school, intending to become a rural family doctor. But then, she says, "I just kind of found my people in surgery. And I honestly think that's how a lot of career decisions are made: We find our tribes. And in medicine there are distinct tribes, distinct personalities between your internal medicine doctors, who are very fastidious, detail-oriented, and happy to tweak medications till kingdom come, and your surgeons, glorified manual laborers who just want to take the giant tumor out and call it a day."

During her surgical residency, she realized, "Holy shit! Surgery is the most wasteful thing I've ever seen in my life. Even for small procedures, we generate these mountains of visible garbage." Andrea took a hiatus from her clinical training and spent a year researching this problem, while completing a master's degree in environmental change and management at Oxford University. She hauled thousands of pounds of garbage from operating rooms in order to analyze it and understand how to reduce waste, and she eventually published a peer-reviewed research paper on her work (she describes her brief foray into the academic publishing process as "its own version of trauma").

While immersed in operating-room garbage, Andrea discovered that this visible form of waste was just the tip of the iceberg. A much bigger problem was hiding in the invisible gases that are pumped into operating rooms to provide anesthesia. If you've ever had surgery, you might remember doctors placing a mask over your nose and mouth before you drifted off to sleep. The mask supplies a constant circuit of gas that keeps you blissfully unconscious during the operation. One widely used type of anesthetic gas, desflurane, is a greenhouse gas that is twenty-five hundred times more harmful than carbon dioxide. And the crazy thing is that doctors don't even need to use it. There are alternative gases that are just as safe and effective for putting patients under during surgery.

Andrea and other doctors raised awareness in the medical community about the outsize impact of desflurane on climate change. At the hospital where Andrea works, the anesthetic machines are now set by default to use a less environmentally destructive gas. She told us that her colleagues "have to make a conscious decision to switch it out if they want to use desflurane. It's also hard to find. There's a tiny stash in some corner of the hospital. It's still there, if someone feels they need it, but they have to really want it." Other hospitals have banned desflurane, but just making it a little hard to get has gone a long way.

Andrea and her colleagues have also moved away from using gas at all in some surgeries. When patients have surgery on their arm or another extremity, doctors can use local anesthesia to freeze the area, rather than grabbing the gas mask and knocking the patient out completely. It turns out this approach not only reduces the environmental impact of surgery but also speeds up the operation and recovery time, enhances patients' satisfaction, and reduces the need for opioid prescriptions afterward. It's what Andrea calls a "triple word score."

When we talked to Andrea, she had just worked almost

thirty-three hours straight, with only a few hours of sleep. Surgeons aren't known for their work-life balance. But while her job isn't easy and requires her to flex both her artistry and humanity to care for individual patients, Andrea told us that her climate work had made her job more interesting. "The truth is that being a surgeon is like being a craftsman, and you master your craft, which is good. But it means that each case is not intellectually stimulating. And that's what you want—you want every surgery to be routine. That's the mastery you're looking for." In contrast, her work on climate change offers her fresh new challenges.

Andrea says that the OR is often viewed as a "sacred cow"; people who haven't spent a lot of time in operating rooms assume everything that happens inside them must be necessary and optimized for patient care. But as a surgeon at a large hospital—a traditional role in a traditional organization—Andrea has intimate knowledge of the OR, which has allowed her to question and change environmentally destructive practices. And she's improved outcomes for patients in the process. So, even if you don't want to switch jobs, it's worth asking where the biggest opportunities might lie to make change in your own workplace. Maybe you can spot the invisible gas that no one else has thought to question.

Bundles of Joy: Kids and Pets

In a 2024 Pew survey, a quarter of young and middle-aged adults without children said that environmental concerns, including climate change, undergirded their decision not to have kids.[47] Some of them had probably seen headlines like "No Babies for the Climate" and "Having Children Is One of the Most Destructive Things You Can Do to the Environment." These media stories cite research led by Seth Wynes, one of JZ's former PhD students. His influential paper showed that having a child is equivalent to taking thirty-seven transatlantic flights per year.[48] But, Seth told us, he never meant to suggest that people should stop having children.

After all, fighting climate change isn't really about saving the planet—this giant spherical rock will be just fine. It's about saving the plants and animals that inhabit the planet, including our own species. And if everyone stopped having babies, our species wouldn't last very long.

Not only that, but Seth shared some good news with us: Since he published his controversial paper, the carbon impact of having children has gone down substantially. "Our calculations assumed a business-as-usual scenario—that if you had a child, your child would keep on emitting at the same pace you did," he explained. But thanks to increases in renewable energy and other climate-friendly policies and innovations, individual emissions are falling and should continue to fall.

Of course, if you've made it this far in the book, you already know that individual emissions hinge in part on where you live and how you get around. So, adding another child to your family will carry relatively light carbon consequences if you live in a place like Portland, which offers clean energy and public transit.

Still, family size does matter. And when it comes to minimizing carbon and maximizing happiness, it looks to us like having one or two children might be a sweet spot. Calculating the hedonic consequences of parenthood isn't easy—we can't randomly assign people to have children. But we can follow them over time and see how their happiness changes as their family grows. One large study found that people experienced a temporary boost in their life satisfaction when they had their first child.[49] They got a smaller boost from having their second child. And by the third child, there was no detectable boost at all.

Overall, parents tend to be slightly happier than people without children, although this difference is remarkably small and often disappears—or even reverses—after controlling for factors like marital status and income.[50] One thing that's clear from the data is that having children doesn't seem to be a *necessary* ingredient for human happiness. So, if becoming a parent doesn't particularly appeal to you, it's totally reasonable to remind meddling relatives that there are lots of low-carbon pathways to a happy life that don't include children.

That said, one reason it's tricky to pinpoint the effect of parenthood on happiness is that children themselves vary so much. Not only that, but parenting a newborn is wildly different than parenting a preteen. When Liz's son, Oliver, was one week old and incapable of sleeping for more than an hour at a time, a sleep-deprived Liz told her husband, "We've ruined our lives." Oliver is now a cheerful twelve-year-old who sleeps late and laughs about this story.

For those of us with kids, adopting a low-carbon approach to parenting might make raising children more enjoyable. In 2024, the US Surgeon General issued a rather dire advisory about the stress and loneliness faced by modern American parents.[51] According to the advisory, 42 percent of parents reported being so stressed that they felt numb, compared to 22 percent of adults without children.

The surgeon general's report points to the need for more community parks and shared spaces where parents can come together and connect. Our friend Azim Shariff told us that he's gotten to know other parents thanks to the shared playroom in his downtown condo building. When kids in the building outgrow their toys, parents donate them. So, the playroom always seems to have a new train set, fire truck, or stuffed animal, delighting Azim's toddler, Illya. And Azim doesn't have to buy Illya new toys of his own, which saves both money and carbon. More important, because Illya has plenty of space to play, Azim's family is happy to stay in their downtown condo, rather than moving to a bigger home in the suburbs—which would carry double the carbon footprint.[52]

Phil Levin, who cofounded Culdesac in Arizona, found a creative way to keep his own housing footprint low, without leaving his home state of California. Before having kids, Phil and his wife, Kristen, built a cluster of small homes around a shared yard in Oakland—and invited their friends to move in. The mini-community, known as Radish, now includes twenty adults and eight little kids. In his Substack, Phil wrote, "People talk about the first year of having a kid as extraordinarily challenging. I feel like a bit of a jerk for saying this, but *it's been much easier than advertised* for us. And we think our living situation plays a huge role in this."[53]

Phil told us that one of the best parts of living at Radish is what he calls "Baby Happy Hour." When the little ones get home from daycare around five thirty p.m., they come out to play in the yard, while the parents catch up with one another. "We'll sip martinis while they play," he told us. There's no scheduling or planning—and no driving. Phil and his friends informally share cars as well as living space, keeping everyone's carbon emissions low. And kids and parents alike feel a warm sense of connection.

Leaving actual human children aside, fur babies may serve as potent catalysts for playfulness and connection. In one delightful study conducted in the UK, a female experimenter went about her daily routine, either with or without a dog in tow.[54] She recorded the number of times people smiled, waved, or chatted with her. Over a ten-day period, a total of sixty-eight strangers interacted with her. Sixty-five of the sixty-eight interactions occurred when she was accompanied by the dog. And when she crossed paths with acquaintances, they were almost three times more likely to engage with her when the dog was present. This finding is particularly notable given that the dog, a Labrador, had been trained not to solicit attention.

Some pets have a fairly large "carbon pawprint," though. A Labrador retriever generates 1.6 tons of carbon per year, mainly because of its carnivorous diet. So, all else being equal, a dog owner who eats a vegan diet has about the same yearly emissions as their petless friend whose fridge is packed with steaks and burgers.[55] Seth has found a sweet spot for himself: He owns an eight-pound Maltese shih tzu named Teddie. Little dogs eat less, so their carbon pawprints are much smaller. A dog Teddie's size typically generates just 0.3 tons of carbon per year, which Seth cuts even further by feeding her an insect-based diet.[56]

Cat lovers can rejoice in knowing that a typical kitty generates just half the emissions of a ten-pound dog.[57] And in a study of nearly twenty thousand Instagram users and two million posts, people who owned cats or dogs appeared happier in their photos than those without pets.[58] Cat owners looked slightly less happy than dog owners, though this could stem from differences in their own personalities rather than in their pets. And people looked happier when they were accompanied by either cats or dogs than by children.

But if you ask JZ, the ultimate joy-inducing carbon-neutral pet is a bunny. Because bunnies eat mostly hay and leafy vegetables, they have the tiniest of carbon pawprints. As a proud bunny parent, JZ loves nothing more than strolling her fluffy bun, Greenwich, around the city in a baby carrier on Saturday afternoons. People passing by often pause, eyes wide, and blurt out, "Oh my god, is that a bunny?" JZ responds, "No, it's just a weird-looking dog." Laughter and conversations ensue. Often, a small crowd swarms around Greenwich, snapping photos, asking to pet the soft little fur-ball, and even poking her to confirm she's not a toy. Once, a line of curious strangers stretched fifty feet down the block, waiting their turn, thinking JZ and Greenwich were street vendors.

Having owned a corgi previously, JZ finds that Greenwich sparks more conversations and interest, spreading joy on every walk. Greenwich will hop onto your lap and perform tricks for treats. She's even litterbox-trained, just like a cat—but much less moody. JZ started eating a more plant-based diet because her fridge was always filled with Greenwich's favorite fruits and vegetables. Greenwich is smart and sassy, and she doesn't bark, making it easy for JZ to work from home. Compared with the Labradors her parents owned, Greenwich doesn't take up much space, enabling JZ to live in a small condo in the heart of downtown Vancouver.

Indeed, our choices about pets and kids are fundamentally intertwined with our decisions about where to live and what kind of work to do. Michelle Armstrong told us that she recently left her job at Arc'teryx, even though she loved it. Arc'teryx was founded in her hometown of Vancouver, but it's now owned by a Chinese company, and as a member of the executive team, Michelle was spending ten days each month in China. She traveled a lot when her two children were young, and, she said, "they didn't like when I was away, but when I was here, they just lived in the present." As her kids became adolescents, though, "they would *dread* my trips. And when I got back, they would tell me for the next two weeks, 'You missed this, you missed that.'" Not only was she racking up outsize emissions by flying around the world, but on a personal level, she told us, "it was unsustainable."

So, Michelle left her job to work as a consultant for other

apparel brands. Gone were the hundred-hour weeks and trips to China. Looking relaxed and well rested, she said, "I couldn't be happier."

For Michelle—and for all of us—creating a livable future means making major life choices that aren't just climate-friendly, but joyful.

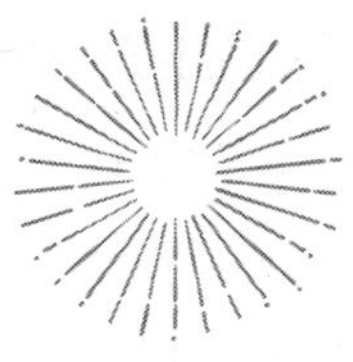

CHAPTER 7

Upward Spirals of Joy

On a sunny day over coffee on Stanford's campus, Ken Gillingham showed his friend Bryan Bollinger a map that he couldn't stop thinking about. After getting interested in solar panels, Ken made a map of the Bay Area showing the houses that had installed them. "I noticed there were clumps of solar installations in some places and not others," Ken explained. As a PhD student in economics, Ken first thought that these clusters could be explained by income, with people in fancier neighborhoods shelling out the cash for solar panels. But then he showed Bryan another map, overlaying income levels, which revealed that some of the clusters were in lower-income neighborhoods. Bryan, a PhD student in marketing, recognized the pattern. His adviser had just found a similar sort of clustering in the adoption of hybrid vehicles. As Bryan and Ken pored over the map, they landed on an exciting conclusion: To them, it looked like solar panels were contagious.

To prove they were right, they dug deeper into the data, looking at how the clusters of solar panels changed over time. If solar panels really were contagious, then Ken and Bryan should observe an upward spiral, whereby solar installations led to more installations, which led to even more installations. And that's exactly what they saw.[1]

"So, if you install solar panels, your neighbor is more likely to install solar panels," Ken told us. In other words, your own, individual actions are just the beginning—they can start an upward spiral that leaves everyone better off. And in this chapter, we'll show you how the dynamics of social change can help you go beyond individual action to influence friends, family, neighbors, business leaders, and policymakers.

You Have to Eat the Mushroom

You've probably heard that if you care about climate change, one of the best things you can do is talk about it. And talking certainly has its place.

For one thing, it can feel comforting to connect with others who share our views on climate change. This insight inspired climate influencer Kristy Drutman to start a YouTube dating show called "Love and Climate." "I have people go on first dates to talk about climate change," Kristy told us. On one date, entrepreneur Noah Hyams told his prospective girlfriend Hope, "I am in a relationship . . . with climate. If you're looking to get in a relationship with me, you're not third-wheeling, but the climate is part of that relationship."[2] While this line might not be a universal winner on the dating scene, Hope told Noah that she shared his view that climate change "affects every aspect of our lives . . . including love and romance." They agreed to a second date.

Thanks to Kristy's dating show, Hope and Noah knew each other's views up front, but it can be uncomfortable to talk about climate change when you're not so sure where the other person stands. According to the spiral of silence theory, people self-censor when they believe their views differ from the views of those around them—which might help to explain why only 5 percent of Americans report talking about climate regularly with friends and family.[3] Sometimes this self-censorship is misplaced. Studies show that people consistently underestimate others' support for climate action. For example, in the US, people estimate that less than 40 percent of their fellow Americans support a carbon tax, but the true figure is closer to 70 percent.[4] So, it can be worth taking the risk of expressing your own pro-climate views even if you don't know exactly how your friends and family will respond.

But sometimes you know all too well how they will respond. JZ's in-laws think the notion that humans cause climate change is "BS." As you can imagine, this makes for tense conversations over Thanksgiving dinner. JZ has been known to hug and kiss flu-ridden friends in the weeks leading up to Thanksgiving, just to have an excuse to skip the holiday. Early on, she tried to marshal all of her knowledge about climate change to get her in-laws on her side. She talked to them about our increasingly hot, dry summers. Her in-laws pointed to recent frigid winters—and then went off on a tangent about volcanoes.

JZ is not alone in failing to persuade her own family members to accept the realities of climate change. These days, she takes solace in research showing that cross-partisan persuasion attempts are rarely effective. While most people—even experts like JZ—aren't all that successful in changing people's minds about polarizing issues like climate change, there might be one exception: In a study conducted in North Carolina, parents reported significantly more concern about climate change after their children learned about this issue in middle school.[5] And this effect was particularly pronounced for parents who started out as climate skeptics. So, children may be unusually effective agents of change when it comes to influencing their parents' attitudes.

But if you're not an adorable eleven-year-old, what can you do? Rather than arguing about the severity or underlying causes of climate change, it can help to focus on solutions. JZ's in-laws still aren't convinced that our hotter, drier summers stem from human-caused climate change—but they took positive action by making renovations to their property to mitigate the growing risk of fires. Because fires spread rapidly, even these small individual actions benefit their neighbors.

And when it comes to these kinds of practical solutions, talking to the people around you can make a real difference. Ken Gillingham and Bryan Bollinger quantified this form of social influence by studying an innovative program in Connecticut called Solarize. The program was created to help communities get discounted solar panels by choosing to work with a single solar company. Local residents volunteered to serve as "solar ambassadors," telling their fellow community members about the benefits of the program. Ken and Bryan found that Solarize dramatically increased panel installations—and most of the uptick stemmed not from the price discount, but from community members influencing one another.[6]

The solar ambassadors were town leaders and others who occupied central spots in their community's social network, and they were invited to volunteer for this reason—regardless of whether they had installed solar panels themselves. But their personal choices mattered. Ambassadors who had installed solar panels in their own homes were significantly more effective at convincing their fellow community members to do so.[7] These ambassadors were practicing what they preached, exhibiting what behavioral scientists call a "credibility-enhancing display." After all, if people really believe that something is beneficial, they should do it themselves.

This principle is deeply rooted in human evolution. Let's say you're walking through the forest with a friend. She points out a colorful mushroom and enthusiastically tells you that it's safe and delicious to eat. If she's wrong, eating it would come at a serious cost, maybe even killing you. So if she really wants to convince you that the mushroom is edible, she should pop it in her own mouth first.

While adopting a new technology or making a lifestyle

change isn't as risky as eating a colorful mushroom, it can still feel pretty high-stakes. So if you want to convince your family, friends, and neighbors to tackle climate change, rather than trying to change their minds, the best place to start is by modeling your own behavior. Any actions you've taken based on the preceding chapters could be the beginning of an upward spiral in your community. Think of yourself as patient (net) zero.

How can you make yourself as contagious as possible? In chapter 2, we described how maximizing EASE could help you stick with low-carbon choices over the long term. Maximizing EASE can also make your own choices more contagious for others. That is, people are more likely to copy your low-carbon choices if you make them look Easy, Attractive, Social, and Eye-catching.

Make It Easy

In an ambitious experiment, researchers studied the power of positive contagion in isolated villages in Honduras.[8] In each village, some households received a public health intervention, which involved face-to-face counseling on issues related to child and maternal health. The counseling produced improvements in knowledge and behavior for these households—but the benefits also spilled over to affect other households that had *not* received the intervention. Importantly, the changes that were easiest to adopt for the households that received the counseling were also more likely to spread to other households in the same village.

So, take a moment to think about any changes you've made in your life to cut back on carbon, and rank these changes from easiest to hardest. Lifestyle changes such as biking more or driving less may be easy in some places and very difficult in others. If you found a lifestyle change easy to make, it's likely that others in your immediate community might have a similar experience. While it's natural to celebrate the hard changes we've made in our lives, talking about the changes that were easy may be more powerful in convincing others to copy us.

Of course, some high-impact changes aren't easy. If you've figured out how to navigate a more complicated change for yourself, then you've broken a trail, which could make it much easier for others to follow in your footsteps. Years ago, our friend Andy Leber installed solar panels in his Columbus, Ohio, home. He told us, "I just learned everything I could about solar. I totally nerded out. I loved it." Then, he started sharing his knowledge. "I have helped probably a couple dozen people go solar, like directly meeting with them, looking at their roof, and having them send me the quotes they get from different solar companies." He describes himself as a "personal concierge" for people who want to go solar or electrify their homes.

Andy has two young children and a full-time job, so we asked him how he fits in all this volunteer work. "If I were doing this twenty hours per week, I would not be alive—it's more like a few hours here and there," he said. "Some people have hobbies. Some people like to unwind at night and just veg out on the couch. I veg out on the couch with my laptop, and I just naturally want to learn more about various things. And if someone sends me a solar quote? That's, like, the most fun thing ever."

Andy has discovered that one of the most valuable things he can do is to help people find a contractor who actually *wants* to do the work, someone who isn't going to give what he calls a "go away" price for it. "I've had contractors come into my house and be like, 'Tell me what you want to do again?' And then they try to talk me out of it. They say electrification is too complicated. They tell me gas is sustainable, it's clean burning—just go with gas. And that's where people who aren't as nerdy about this as me, they will just want to walk away. They don't want to spend hours figuring out how to do it. They just want to do it." Andy makes it easier for them, in part by finding contractors who are pro-electrification.

So, if you've hired a contractor to electrify your home—by installing solar panels or a heat pump or replacing a gas stove with an electric one—simply sharing their name with others can make the process much easier. And if you have a nerdy streak, embrace your inner Andy and consider sharing your own skills and knowledge. Even something as simple as sharing what you learned while shopping for your new EV can save your friends and family enough time that they might just follow your lead.

Make It Attractive

If there were a Crayola box for climate communication, it would be stuffed with bleak colors like Smokestack Gray and Deforestation Brown. But offering vibrant, appealing images of low-carbon lifestyle choices is important if we want more people to adopt them. As a climate influencer, Kristy Drutman showcases her own choices with lifestyle vlogs that focus on sustainable fashion and thrifting: "I show people the outfits I'm wearing, that I'm eating a plant-based meal, and just kind of walk people through my day. People have enjoyed watching those because they're like, 'Oh, this is the kind of lifestyle I would want.'"

Jay Van Bavel, a prominent NYU professor with a large social media following, shared his own joyful lifestyle changes on X (formerly Twitter). He announced that he was aiming for "10% retirement," in part by cutting back on travel to conferences. With his newfound time affluence, Jay wrote, "I am saying yes to better sleep, to more exercise, and to being more present with my family, friends, collaborators, and students." He challenged his colleagues to join him in getting off the "academic hamster wheel." Other academics chimed in to say that they, too, were cutting back on time-consuming conference travel, partly because of its high carbon costs. As Jay put it, "This will all come much easier if we do it together."

And social media isn't the only avenue for influence. After moving into a new home, Ken Gillingham put his research into action by installing solar panels and chatting with curious neighbors about their benefits. Sure enough, some of his neighbors installed their own panels. To make solar panels especially attractive, Ken has a pro tip: If you live in a place that suffers from occasional extended power outages and you have batteries that store your solar energy, invite your neighbors over for a shower the next time the power goes out. Nothing makes solar more attractive than a hot shower during a blackout.

Sharing these compelling positive experiences is important, according to Gregg Sparkman, a professor at Boston College who studies the psychology of social change. He told us that when it comes to adopting new environmentally friendly technologies like solar panels or EVs, people tend to focus on the potential downsides. "People are going to focus on that one news story about an EV catching fire on the freeway, or someone being stranded because of range issues," he said. "So, to drown out those examples, you need ten times as many people being like, 'This EV is amazing. I love it.'"

In her social media posts, Kristy Drutman emphasizes how much she enjoys her own low-carbon lifestyle—an approach that stands out from that of many other climate communicators. "My tone is a lot less serious, but that doesn't mean I'm not serious about the issue. I'm just making it more approachable. I talk as though I were talking to a friend or family member. I'm not like, 'Why don't you care? You're what's wrong with the world because you don't care!' I think that tone is overdone and people aren't going to respond to it anymore." Shame and guilt may motivate some people, but positive emotions can also be powerful tools for spurring social change.

Environmental activist Etelle Higonnet agrees with Kristy. She told us that adopting a warm, appealing tone can also be powerful when it comes to spurring change from companies. We usually think of boycotts or shaming campaigns on social media as the ways to inspire change, but these aren't the only strategies.

"For example, let's say Lavazza is not doing a great job on the environment, but they have this one coffee that supports a rainforest project in Brazil. If you buy that coffee, you're giving even a bad company reinforcement for the good stuff they do," Etelle said. "Another thing that's fun to do is to buy exactly what you've always bought, but every time you do it, take a picture of yourself, put it on Instagram, and send it to the company saying, 'Get deforestation out of my coffee. I love you and I want you to change.' It's like you're coming from a place of being a loyal customer who wants the company to do better."

Aman Singh, who led sustainability communications for Walmart, told us that this kind of post catches the eye of marketing teams, which closely monitor social media. If you want to maximize your effectiveness in getting companies to change, Aman said, "Don't *just* use social media for complaining, but also for validating some of the actions companies are taking." These forms of validation can help sustainability professionals like Aman advocate for more positive changes in their companies.

Offering carrots, rather than just sticks, can be particularly powerful—and joyful—when it comes to small businesses. In Santa Barbara, California, a local environmental group organized a "carrot mob," akin to a flash mob, of consumers who visited a local café one day in January. The café had made a series of positive changes to enhance sustainability, and the carrot mob was created to applaud the café's efforts and encourage them to take another big step forward. One organizer dressed in a carrot costume, and a band played. More than four hundred people visited the coffee shop that day, generating fourteen hundred dollars in extra profits for the café, enabling them to invest in energy efficiency upgrades. Think of it as a "buycott" rather than a boycott.

At first, the idea of doling out carrots for minor victories seemed wrong to Kathy Kuntz, who leads the Office of Energy and Climate Change in Dane County, Wisconsin. But as a local policymaker, she didn't have a lot of sticks at her disposal. In Wisconsin, local governments have relatively little real power (specifically, they lack regulatory authority). "We can't do mandates, so it's carrots and more carrots. And really it should be carrot cake, because then it's got frosting, and it's way more delicious than just a pile of carrots." To harness the power of carrot cake, Kathy created a Climate Champions award, which recognizes organizations that have taken positive actions in tackling climate change. The awards have gone to an architecture firm that worked on decarbonizing buildings and a dental office that became the first in the nation to go carbon neutral. As Kathy puts it, "We look for things that folks are doing right and give them credit for this."

And you don't need to be a policymaker to dole out awards. If you belong to a student organization, a neighborhood group, or a church, you could create an annual Climate Champions award to honor a local business that's making progress on climate. "We've done work inside companies, where the way to get the CEO excited about the sustainability goals is to let him accept an award for something that the company has done," Kathy said. "Then he comes back, really fired up and saying, 'We need to do more of this—we're not doing enough!'"

According to cognitive dissonance theory, receiving praise can motivate us to live up to it. We want to avoid the twinge of discomfort we often feel when our behavior doesn't align with the way others see us. In one study, adults in Germany answered questions about their current pro-environmental behavior, and then some of them received praise for doing better than others.[9] Although the individuals who received praise were actually chosen at random, they subsequently reported higher intentions to take future pro-environmental actions, compared with those who were told they were average or worse than average.

Awards can also foster competition. After the city of Middleton, Wisconsin, received a Climate Champions award in 2021, Kathy heard from a leader in the nearby city of Sun Prairie. He complained, "Every time I get an email from anyone in the city of Middleton, it says 'We're a Dane County Climate Champion!' at the bottom of the email. It's kind of annoying."

Kathy asked him, "Don't you think you'd be less annoyed if it said that in *your* email signature?" The city of Sun Prairie stepped up its game, hired a new sustainability manager, and soon won its own Climate Champions award.

These awards are simple and practically free. "What organizations get from us is a decal they put in their email and a sticker for a window," Kathy explained. She recalls one of her mentors telling her, "Kathy, clapping for someone doesn't cost you anything."

The carrot cake approach involves letting go of perfection while offering praise for progress. This flies in the face of what Kathy learned from working in the energy efficiency world. "We were very careful not to give people incentives until we knew they bought the efficient bulbs. It's very transactional. And of course, transactional things are not what usually give us bliss." So, she told us, now "we're learning to lean in and meet people where they are, celebrate whatever tiny things they're already doing. Then we talk about how we can help make it easier for them to do the next things."

This approach didn't always come naturally to her. "We used to do these surveys where we would ask people, 'Have you done something in the last year to save energy?' Everyone says yes, and invariably a huge portion of them say they recycle. As an efficiency person, my reaction is like, 'That doesn't even count. That's not an efficiency thing. No.' But I've learned to say, 'That is awesome that you're recycling. Have you also thought about how you might take the bus?'" Her style echoes a fundamental principle of improv: To create connection, respond to your partner with "Yes, and . . ." Instead of negating the assumption that recycling is tied to energy efficiency, Kathy takes it as a starting point and offers more impactful actions as the next steps.

Still, Kathy sometimes encounters resistance from people who find the carrot cake approach too sweet. "People say, 'I think we should be calling out the bad guys.' I'm like, 'Yes, if it worked, I would be doing it, because what I care about is results.'" But she's found that making climate action attractive is what produces results.

She told us that in the world of climate action, "Happiness is for many people the antithesis of what we're doing. And I'm like, 'Okay, but if the future you want people to live in is dull and boring and all about suffering, who's going to lean into that?"

Make It Social

To avoid the carbon costs of flying, Gregg Sparkman would take long solo journeys by train to attend academic conferences. But as a graduate student at Stanford, he found a more social—and joyful—strategy. He rented a van and drove with four colleagues from Palo Alto, California, to a major conference in New Orleans. "We just made it really fun. We stopped at the Grand Canyon. We stopped in Vegas. And this approach quintupled my impact. Instead of it being just me not flying, it was me and four other people, packed in a van, driving through the night—but also finding a lot of fun in the experience." When they arrived at the conference, they got a lot of questions from friends. "Everyone was surprised that we had driven there. People asked, 'Why didn't you fly?!'" Gregg had gotten these questions before, but now his four friends could field them, too, creating potential ripple effects through the conference.

Looking back, though, Gregg does have one regret. "Some of my friends were unprepared to explain the environmental reasons" for the road trip, he told us. If he were to do it again, Gregg would end the road trip by making sure his friends knew just how much carbon they had saved. That way, when they were chatting with people at the conference, they could emphasize not only the beauty of the Grand Canyon but also the environmental benefits of driving together, rather than flying.

Ideally, we want to bring our friends along for the ride—but also equip them with knowledge that can make them more effective agents of change. So, if this book has resonated with you, you could organize a book club to discuss it with friends (you'll find ideas and materials for book clubs at happyclimate.org). As well as broadening your reach, sharing the ideas in this book with friends can make it easier and more joyful to think through the lifestyle changes that each of you could make to cut carbon and get happier.

Friends can stress-test each other's plans, identifying the obstacles that are likely to pop up and helping to overcome them. To promote physical exercise, city councils in the UK invited some of their staff members to make plans to walk more in daily life.[10] The plans included detailed "implementation intentions," in the form of if-then statements like "If it's not raining, then I will walk to work." Meanwhile, other staff members were also asked to make an if-then plan, but instead of doing it on their own, they hammered out the plan with a friend, spouse, or other partner. Lots of research suggests that concrete if-then plans can help people turn their vague goals into lasting action. And this simple approach did help. One month later, people who were instructed to make a plan walked about 14 percent more frequently than their colleagues who had not made a plan.

But people who made the plan along with a friend or other partner walked about 47 percent more frequently.

In addition to helping each other make stronger plans, friends can hold each other accountable. In Chile, researchers wanted to help people save money. They gave some people a basic savings account and assigned them to participate in a weekly Savings Group meeting, in which group members held each other accountable for meeting their individual savings goals. Others got a basic savings account but no weekly meetings. The researchers found that participants who were assigned to a Savings Group saved almost four times as much money.[11]

Of course, attending weekly meetings doesn't sound so enjoyable to us. But a follow-up study showed that just receiving simple text messages about how others in the group were doing was sufficient to produce similar benefits. So, if you want to implement the ideas in this book, consider not only holding a book club to hammer out if-then plans but also making a WhatsApp group to check in with everyone afterward.

This approach may even help your friends feel like they can do hard things. In one experiment, young adults were asked to choose math problems to solve, which varied in difficulty.[12] They overwhelmingly preferred the less challenging problems (people like easy things!). But when they observed a peer tackling the harder problems, they became a little more likely to choose hard problems, too. And let's face it: Climate change is a hard problem.

When she was just a teenager, Vanessa Timmer stumbled

onto the power of social contagion for tackling hard problems. As a high school student in the early 1990s, she cofounded a group called the Environmental Youth Alliance. "It grew from the sixteen of us to fourteen thousand young people within a couple of years. And it was pre-internet!" she told us. Now, as the leader of a major nonprofit organization called OneEarth Living, Vanessa harnesses what she learned about maximizing contagion. "We found that one of the most effective ways to move sustainable living forward is to do it through groups. So, we work in neighborhoods and workplaces. And we see promise in engaging sports clubs, faith groups, communities of interest, book clubs, and community centers. We think of places where people are already gathering in order to get those upward spirals started."

A similar hyper-social approach underlies the work of an organization called Rewiring America, which is successfully electrifying households, businesses, and communities across the United States. As vice president of communications and creative strategy at Rewiring America, Sarah Lazarovic takes her work home with her. To encourage her friends and neighbors to invest in heat pumps, she told us, "I throw heat pump parties. I invite anybody who wants to come, and we make dorky heat pump cocktails and ugly heat pump cookies, and everyone can just ask all their questions."

And, she says, it works. "I think there are about ten people already on my street who have gotten heat pumps. It just makes me feel so good. And that's what I do, writ large at my job." Rewiring America trains people to serve as "electric coaches."

Sarah told us, "One woman invited a bunch of people over to her garage to learn about the Inflation Reduction Act and have a sing-along." Inspired by these parties, Sarah and her colleagues are creating cookie kits. "You get lightning cookie kits mailed to you with frosting" so you can invite your friends over to make cookies and chat about electrification.

For folks who are stuck with gas stoves because they rent their home or can't afford an electric stove, Sarah loves inexpensive induction hot plates. "We're launching a whole kit. We will send people a hot plate—plus a soup kit—and it's, like, a hundred bucks total, and then they can make soup for their neighbors. It's about community and joy."

For Sarah and her colleagues, Rewiring America isn't just about electricity, but also about social connection. "The wires are literal, but they also have to be metaphorical, because you're powering your neighbor. If the grid goes down, it's a community resilience story. We have to have that social cohesion. We all have to be in this deep web of interconnection, so that if my power goes out, you're helping me."

Make It Eye-Catching

The more visible you can make your pro-climate behavior, the more likely it is to spread. Ken Gillingham quantified the power of visibility by creating 3D maps of rooftop solar displays across Connecticut.[13] His team identified the households that could see each set of panels, and then analyzed whether these households were more likely to install their own panels. As it turned out, visibility mattered—a lot. Just being able to see a set of solar panels increased the likelihood of installing them by nearly as much as getting a six-hundred-dollar discount.

In Harrisburg, Pennsylvania, the Tree of Life Lutheran Church made the most of its highly visible location on a busy road.[14] The congregation had been discussing installing solar panels for years, when one couple stepped up and offered to foot the bill. The church installed solar panels in 2023. The nine hundred members of the church congregation see the panels every Sunday, but so, too, do drivers of more than ten thousand vehicles that pass the church each day. The pastor, Reverend Richard Geib, said, "People are seeing the solar panels as an example of a green solution and a positive expression of what it means to be the church."

If you live on a busy street, or in a central part of your neighborhood, you could be an intersection influencer, spurring the rest of your community toward low-carbon choices. Let's say you bought a bright red EV and you love it. Consider showing it off by parking it on the street where others can see it, rather than driving it straight into your garage every day.

Less expensive lifestyle choices can also spread rapidly, thanks to the magic of visibility. In the twin cities of Minneapolis and Saint Paul, researchers tried to figure out what motivated people to join a bike-share program called Nice Ride Minnesota.[15] Surprisingly, living near a bike-share station or having previous biking experience didn't really matter. What did matter was the number of other people nearby who participated in the program. So, simply joining a bike-share program and cycling around your neighborhood can encourage those around you to adopt this ultralow-carbon form of transportation.

Biking, driving an EV, and installing solar panels are highly visible forms of pro-climate behavior, but other actions—like driving less and reducing energy use—are hard for others to see. And these invisible behaviors are much less contagious than highly visible ones. So, an interesting challenge lies in making these climate-friendly behaviors more observable. In New York and Massachusetts, people who rent their homes or can't afford pricey panels are able to harness solar power by purchasing it from others in their area. MySunBuddy is a solar marketplace that pairs people who want solar energy with those whose panels produce more energy than they need.[16] This peer-to-peer network expands the number of people who have access to solar power—but unfortunately, these new solar users are rendered invisible. So, MySunBuddy sent these customers "Green Reports," documenting their use of solar energy, which were designed to be shared on social media. These Green Reports made not only their choice of clean energy visible, but the whole prospect of peer-to-peer solar more appealing to potential customers.

Heat pumps are another innovation that can be self-defeatingly unobtrusive, tucked away behind bushes on the side of a house. Perhaps because of this, they tend not to be very contagious. So, if you've got a heat pump, it's worth thinking of ways to pimp your pump. Behavior change expert Gregg Sparkman suggests emblazoning your heat pump with the logo of your favorite sports team. You could also cover it in joyful

Christmas lights—and leave the lights on all year, so people notice them every time they walk past your house at night. If nothing else, Gregg suggests celebrating your new heat pump installation with a simple yard sign displaying a message like "I recently installed a heat pump. Ask me anything!" Or you can take a page from Sarah's book and wear a heat pump costume for Halloween. This unusual costume pretty much guarantees your neighbors will ask what you're wearing, giving you a chance to talk about heat pumps and enjoy a friendly conversation with people who otherwise might have walked by you.

And even if your neighbors don't install heat pumps of their own, your visible action can spur them to adopt other pro-climate behaviors. When researchers in Australia studied how environmentally friendly actions spread through neighborhoods, they found that the more people in a neighborhood adopted a visible low-carbon behavior, the more likely others in the area were to adopt the same behavior—and other low-carbon behaviors, too.[17]

Not only that, but joy itself appears to be contagious. In a remarkable study, researchers tracked the social networks and happiness levels of more than five thousand people in Framingham, Massachusetts.[18] They found that happiness can spread from one person to another within neighborhoods. In fact, if you become happier, a friend who lives within one mile of you is likely to get happier, too. And the effect is even stronger for next-door neighbors, perhaps because they see each other more often. So, taking a joyful approach to tackling climate change can help others around you lead happier lives, too.

Changing the System

As part of a 2024 survey, people in seventy-seven nations were asked who they think has had the most impact addressing climate change in their own country: the government, the United Nations, big business, campaigners and activists, or faith and community leaders. In nine out of ten countries, the government was seen as the most impactful.[19]

At the same time, though, a lot of people see politics as anything but joyful. Nathaniel Stinnett, who's known as the "voting guru" of the environmental movement, told us, "I think a lot of people in their hearts are very cynical about politics. They say, 'Politicians do whatever it takes to get elected, and they don't care about me.'"

Rather than arguing with this concern, Nathaniel takes a "Yes . . . and" approach, encouraging folks to "take their cynicism one step further. If you think that all politicians care about is winning elections, then that means you are the *only* thing that matters. And especially in the United States, where it's a matter of public record whether you vote or not, politicians literally have a list by name and street address of people who vote and don't vote in their districts."

Nathaniel has seen this list firsthand. In 2013, he served as the campaign manager for one of the top candidates in Boston's race for mayor. "We wanted to talk about climate change," he said. "But we polled voters, and they cared about potholes and public schools, like most people do in local elections." And this apparent apathy about climate change extended beyond Boston's mayoral race. "Whether I was working on a US Senate race, or a city council race, or anything in between, we would poll voters and almost none of them listed climate or environmental issues as a top priority. No matter how great an environmental champion the candidate you're working with is, if voters don't deeply care about a particular issue, you can't spend your time talking about it."

Then, Nathaniel discovered something that changed his whole perception of the problem. After examining polls of voters, he turned to data from a group of people he and his colleagues usually ignored: nonvoters. Among this large—and largely overlooked—group, many people reported caring deeply about climate change. "That made me think: I wonder if the climate movement has a turnout problem rather than a persuasion problem." There were more than enough people who cared about climate change, but they weren't voting, and so they were invisible to politicians. As a result of this eureka moment, Nathaniel started the Environmental Voter Project, an organization that has identified more than eight million nonvoting environmentalists and harnessed the best tools of behavioral science to turn them into consistent "super-voters."

Voting, at its core, is an act of generosity. After all, you have to give up some of your own time and bandwidth for the greater good. While this might seem like a sacrifice, Liz's research shows that engaging in acts of generosity can promote happiness.[20] And she's discovered that there are some key catalysts that turn good deeds into good feelings. The most important catalyst is knowing that you are actually making a difference.

Unfortunately, in federal elections, it can be hard to feel like your one little vote matters. But in local politics, it's much easier to see that you can have an impact. "In Nebraska, where utilities are publicly owned, if you change the membership of a five-person public utility board in an election where only fifteen hundred people vote, you can shut down a coal-fired power plant," Nathaniel told us. "Or, in a little parish in the bayou of Louisiana, if you vote to change the makeup of the city council, they might be able to change the zoning code and literally stop a petrochemical plant from being built. You can make an enormous difference."

Liz used to spend her time obsessing over federal elections, while entirely ignoring local ones. This changed because of a New Year's resolution. And it wasn't even her own. Liz and her friends play an annual New Year's Eve game in which each person writes down their resolution on a piece of paper. Everyone puts their own resolution into a hat, and then each person draws one and must guess which of their friends wrote it. If they fail to guess the resolution's author, they have to adopt the resolution as their own. Liz drew the resolution "Get more involved in local politics" and couldn't guess which of her friends had written it. So, Liz took the time to learn about local political issues, and she advocated for schools to prepare better for natural disasters. The whole endeavor turned out to be much more satisfying than she had anticipated (sometimes scientists forget to apply the lessons from their research to their own lives!). She surprised her friends by showing up on local TV news talking about issues in the community.

JZ, too, got involved in local politics, but for her, this transition happened when she received Canadian citizenship. Having grown up in China, she had never voted in an election before, so when the next local election rolled around, JZ didn't just plan to vote; she requested interviews with the candidates. One of them ignored her request, but a first-time candidate named Terry Yung responded the very next day. She met him in person and grilled him for half an hour. Liz—who had taken voting and citizenship for granted—was stunned. But JZ told her, you don't hire someone for an important job without interviewing them first. Terry Yung was surprised, too, and seemed nervous during the interview. But he managed to impress JZ. Two weeks later, Yung won the election by just 1,161 votes, and JZ's vote was one of them.

Focusing on local elections—even seemingly trivial ones—is a hallmark of the Environmental Voter Project's theory of change. "The only way to turn a nonvoter into a voter is to get them to vote in an election," Nathaniel said. "That's it. And so we gobble up elections even when they seem objectively unimportant. No one is going to be like, 'Let's spend money mobilizing people for this special Public Utility Board primary.' But we love that stuff." So if you care about climate change, voting in *every* election is a great New Year's resolution. As Nathaniel put it, "Simply by being a voter you become a first-class citizen," someone politicians have no choice but to see and care about.

To scale up your impact, the next step is to get your like-minded friends and family out to vote in every election, too. Rather than just pestering them to vote, think about how you can make it easier for them, perhaps by offering neighbors a ride to the polls, or looking up the addresses of the closest polling places for your friends.

Andy Leber took this a step further, by making it easy for his fellow community members to see where local candidates stood on issues related to climate change. Before local elections, he and his friends sent each candidate a questionnaire asking about their positions on key climate issues. Then, they printed up postcards sharing each candidate's answers. "We didn't endorse anybody. We just provided information," he told us. "We live in a world where local news coverage is dying. So, people were grateful that we had collected this information and distributed it." Taking even one hour to look up each candidate's position on a couple of key issues relevant to climate change and then emailing a brief summary to your colleagues, book club, or parent-teacher association could make it easier for everyone to support pro-climate candidates.

You can also make voting more attractive and social by inviting friends to a party on the night of the next local election. You could hold it at your house, or kick it up a notch and work with a community organization to hold a party near a polling place (for ideas and rules about how to do this, go to happy climate.org). Multiple field experiments show that holding festive gatherings near polling places can increase voter turnout, particularly among young voters and people of color.[21] In fact, turning voting into a community celebration—with free food, dancing, and a DJ—may be more cost-effective than less joyful strategies like phone-banking.

And when you score a victory for the climate, it's worth taking time to celebrate with friends. After a pro-electrification ballot initiative got passed in his town, Andy framed the mailer that he and his friends had sent out, and gave one to each of those friends. "Every time I look at this," he told us, holding up the framed mailer, "I just think, Wow, you know what? Sometimes the stuff that we do has a positive outcome. Just seeing that as a visual reminder, and celebrating the small victories is really important." This reminder of success helps motivate Andy and his friends to keep at it.

When it comes to voting, Gregg Sparkman recommends making your own civic action as eye-catching as possible. "Just being in the voting booth by yourself isn't going to cut it," he told us. If you want to encourage other people to vote, "you need the yard sign. You need the bumper sticker. You need the T-shirt."

Voting is essential, but it isn't the only way to influence climate policy. When Isak Drangstveit was in fifth grade, he learned about climate change in school. "So," he told us, "I asked my dad about it. He was like, 'Yeah, this is a real thing, but you shouldn't have to worry about it, Isak. It's okay; we're working on it.' And I didn't accept that as a reasonable answer." Isak began leading sustainability initiatives at school in his small hometown, the village of Waunakee, Wisconsin. In high school, he joined the Dane County Youth Environmental Committee, which brought together kids from across the county. Meeting kids from other towns and hearing about their progress made him realize that Waunakee was falling behind.

At one of the meetings, Isak got to chat with Kathy Kuntz,

who was attending on behalf of Dane County's Office of Energy and Climate Change. Kathy told Isak he was right about his hometown: While other parts of the county were making real progress on climate change, Waunakee was lagging behind. "She told me I could do something about it," Isak recalls. "It was kind of insane. I was like, 'Oh, Kathy, I can't vote. They're not going to listen to me.'" But Kathy told him that just showing up at the local village board meetings could make a difference.

So, Isak showed up. He asked the village board to create a sustainability committee to help Waunakee catch up with surrounding towns. They shook his hand, smiled, and thanked him for asking about this issue. He was frustrated, though, when he didn't see action. Kathy told us this was the Midwestern version of saying, "Shut up and go away." But Isak stayed for the whole meeting. And he kept coming back. He gave a presentation to the village board, and six months later, the board approved the creation of a sustainability committee, with two spots reserved for young people, as Isak had asked. "It felt amazing," he told us. "Because I actually got to do something."

"I encourage the youth especially to be focused locally because they can see their impact," Kathy told us. "There were a ton of other folks lobbying legislators at the state and federal level, but really nobody was lobbying the village board of Waunakee—except Isak. And it worked."

In order to have a real and joyful impact at the local level, it's essential to know what to ask for—and whom to ask. "I think one of the biggest frustrations people have is knocking on the wrong door with the wrong ask," Rebecca Alty told us. As mayor of Yellowknife, the capital city of Canada's Northwest Territories, Rebecca has been on the front lines of climate change, confronting disastrous floods and fires in her community. Sitting in her office—with a pair of cross-country skis in the corner—she told us, "Everybody thinks the mayor is this all-powerful person, a bit like a dictator." But in Yellowknife, as in many other communities, the mayor has just one vote on issues facing the city. A team of city councillors works closely with the mayor, and each of them gets one vote, too. "Everybody wants to meet with the mayor, but not everyone thinks to reach out to their councillor."

Vanessa Timmer, the leader of OneEarth Living, agrees with Rebecca—and takes this a step further. She thinks people who care about climate change should "adopt a city councillor." You, your neighborhood, or your environmental club can pick a councillor and celebrate them when they do something great by showing up at council meetings to support them. Or simply invite them to your neighborhood barbecue or your book club. Events like these are attractive opportunities for your councillor to connect with voters, so they're likely to say yes, especially if you keep inviting them.

Building these longer-term relationships can be powerful, but if you only want to devote a few hours per year to tackling climate policy, Rebecca and other leaders told us there's one time of the year that matters more than any other. And that's budget season. "It's actually one of the times we rarely hear from people," Rebecca said. She thinks many people feel like, "'Oh, I'm not very good at math. I don't understand how this works.'"

But she says their reluctance to engage is misplaced. "I'm not asking you to balance the budget, but I want to hear what your priorities are." She suggests writing an email at the start of budget season saying that you want better bike paths and you're willing to pay more taxes to get them.

If you're going to email your local politicians, send the message in your own words, from your own account. Marianne Alto, the mayor of British Columbia's capital city of Victoria, told us she gets a lot of auto-generated emails. "I might get nine thousand emails on Climate Issue X. When I try to reply, I don't get an actual person." Instead, she said, she gets an auto-response from the bot that delivered the message. "And so for me, that's meaningless. Utterly meaningless. Because all it takes is for someone to go onto a website, add their name, and press send." But a small amount of effort goes a long way. "It's much more effective for me to get a hundred emails, each of which is actually from a person. And although they have the same message, it's written slightly differently, and I can reply. That is much more compelling and effective than anything that comes from a robot mailer," Marianne said.

Finally—and most important—it's essential to devote your energy to initiatives that can make a real difference. So many issues, from eliminating plastic bags to buying organic food, have wound up under the banner of climate change when they don't really belong there. "I'll get these letters during Earth Week saying we should pick up litter," Rebecca told us. "I agree, let's all pick up litter. But picking up litter isn't going to stop climate change."

So, what really matters? In a study evaluating climate policies in forty-one countries over the past two decades, researchers found that one of the strategies that had the biggest impact was implementing a carbon tax.[22] The core idea of a carbon tax is that businesses and consumers should pay for the carbon they create.

Unfortunately, taxes sound anything but joyful. In one study, people were asked to make a hypothetical choice between a bond that would pay $400 per year with $100 chopped off for taxes, or a tax-free bond that would pay $300 per year. Although people would get the same $300 payoff either way, nearly 80 percent preferred the tax-free bond.[23] This study suggests that people would prefer to forgo $100 entirely, rather than giving it to the government. So, a key challenge lies in making the carbon tax more delightful. In some provinces of Canada, the government experimented with rebranding the carbon tax as the "Canada Carbon Rebate," with most of the money that was collected going back to individual Canadians. A family with two children in Ontario, for example, would receive more than a thousand dollars deposited directly into their bank account from this carbon rebate. And Liz's research suggests that financial windfalls can significantly improve life satisfaction.[24]

Besides the carbon tax (sorry, carbon *rebate*!), other policies that have turned out to be effective include phasing out coal plants, changing building codes (to require lower-carbon heating), and subsidizing renewable energy by providing rebates for heat pumps and EVs.[25] And combining multiple pro-climate policies makes the biggest difference of all. To test out your own ideas about what bouquet of policies might work best, you can play with an amazing simulator called En-ROADS, created by researchers at MIT (you'll find a link to En-ROADS at happy climate.org).[26]

Pushing government leaders to adopt these policies can make a big difference, but if you want to have an even bigger impact, you could consider running for office yourself. Marianne Alto told us, "It was never my childhood dream to become the mayor of Victoria." But by getting involved as a city councillor and then as mayor, she's helped to make Victoria one of the world's leading cities in tackling climate change.

Like Marianne, Rebecca didn't see herself in the mayor's office. In fact, she only got involved in politics to help a friend who was running for city council. Rebecca told us that her friend asked her to serve as campaign manager. "I didn't know what that was. But I said, 'Yes. I can figure it out.'" Part of figuring it out involved attending a campaign school for women. There were about ten women, and the school's director asked each of them whether they were running for office or helping someone else run. "We go around the table, and we're all like, 'we're helping,' 'we're helping,' 'we're helping.'" The director was dismayed. She told them, "If women only *help*, we'll never get women elected."

"It just kind of got me thinking about it," Rebecca said. "So, I broke the news to my friend: 'Actually, I can't be your campaign manager. I'm going to be your competitor.'" Luckily, they both won spots on the city council, and Rebecca assured us, "We've lived happily ever after."

After two terms on council, Rebecca ran for mayor, and won. "I think it's like any job," she told us. "There's good days and hard days. But at the municipal level, you are able to make changes and see the impact."

Be the Edge Fish

Fish don't have mayors, or CEOs, or sustainability managers—but they are surprisingly adept at what ecologists call "collective evasion maneuvers." When we feel like climate change is too big a problem for us to escape, we enjoy watching videos showing sardines successfully evading sea lions (see happyclimate.org for one of our favorites).[27] Faced with a giant problem—a hungry sea lion—schools of six-inch sardines miraculously manage to stay alive.

Scientists have dissected this miracle, as scientists love to do. It turns out that fish on the outer edge of the school—both up front and on the sides—make this miracle happen. Their position on the outer edge enables them to detect the threat posed by the sea lion, and to dart away. If only one fish makes a move, the school doesn't change direction, and all of them remain vulnerable. But there seems to be a critical threshold, whereby the whole group can change course rapidly and elude the sea lion. One study found that if 25 percent of fish switch direction, the entire school will follow with mind-blowing speed.[28]

And a remarkably similar tipping point has been discovered among our own species.[29] By conducting carefully controlled experiments, Damon Centola and his colleagues have shown that when 25 percent of people alter their behavior, it can trigger widespread changes in social norms. This finding flies in the face of traditional economic thought, which suggests the tipping point should be 51 percent.

It only takes a quarter of the population to change social norms because of the high costs of falling out of sync with others. Take, for example, the way people greet new acquaintances. When Liz was in college, she met her roommate's father, who came from a French background and was accustomed to "la bise," a traditional greeting that entails two brief kisses on each cheek. Liz was not expecting this greeting, so she moved her face the wrong way, and ended up kissing her roommate's dad on the lips, in front of his whole family.

After this single encounter, Liz became more attuned to any nonverbal signs that someone was moving in for la bise. Liz's experience fits with Damon's research showing that people are highly sensitive to changes in others' behavior. We're like the fish: When 25 percent of individuals change direction, the rest of the school can quickly follow. Because of this fundamental property of behavior, change isn't linear. And this is good news for tackling the climate crisis. After all, we don't have time for linear change. But as Al Gore put it, "When the culture shifts, when consciousness changes, everything else can change rapidly—faster than people think."[30]

Damon told us that this rapid shift is often preceded by a discouraging period in which change occurs very, very slowly. "If you're right at the twenty-one or twenty-two percent mark, it can be really frustrating," he said. "It's almost like a failed enterprise, or at least one that's insufficient." You may feel like your own positive behaviors will never spread through the rest of the population. "But what you don't know is that you're just on the cusp of something really, truly amazing."

Welcome to the cusp. Approaching climate change from a place of joy can be contagious. By adopting a climate-friendly lifestyle, you can be the edge fish, leading others in the same direction and helping to evade the most important existential threat of our time.

ACKNOWLEDGMENTS

When it comes to happiness, almost nothing matters more than feeling a sense of connection and gratitude to other people. And writing this book gave us both, in spades.

We are grateful to the effervescent Briar Goldberg, whose early enthusiasm for our idea helped fuel our desire to pursue it.

As we began talking to literary agents, they all told us the same thing: "Books on climate change don't sell." But Margo Beth Fleming of the Brockman Agency was undaunted. She understood our idea from our very first phone call—and her belief in this book helped to make it a reality. Over and over again, she went beyond our expectations, helping to sharpen our thinking while gently guiding us to make smart choices. We appreciate you so much, Margo.

Thanks to Margo, we got the chance to talk to multiple

potential editors who were interested in this book. After one of these calls, we turned to each other and said, *"Wow!"* We had just spoken to Tracy Behar, who would become our editor. Her vision for this book not only matched our own, but helped to elevate it. At the time, Tracy had recently become the president of Avery and Tarcher at Penguin Random House. So, we figured she would be very busy, but that getting even a little of her brilliant attention would be worth it. And yet somehow, she made us feel like we were her only authors, turning around drafts for us with dazzling speed. Her insightful edits and warm encouragement made writing this book a joy. In the world of publishing, Tracy is the GOAT.

As we worked on each chapter, we received invaluable research support from Charul Maheshka, Ariya Kosivisutte, and especially Chastity Leong Ka See, who relentlessly chased down facts and assisted us in creating the figures.

We asked some of the smartest people we know for feedback on this book, including Kirstin Appelt, David Hardisty, Hannah Ritchie, and Sam Yagan. We were especially lucky to get feedback from one of our favorite writers of all time, Mandy Catron. Despite being busy with twin toddlers and her own writing, Mandy made time to help us with every single chapter in this book. As our writing coach, she enabled us to find words for the ideas bouncing around in our heads.

The best part of this whole project was getting to talk to fascinating people who shared their stories and insights with us. We interviewed more than eighty people for this book, and many of their names appear in its pages—but we would also like to thank all the others, who shaped our thinking behind the scenes, including: Max Besbris, Lauren Bruggemans, Raphael Calel, Kookai Chaimahawong, Frances Chen, Gracen Chungath, Emilie Comeau-Sinclair, Alex Da Silva, Rebecca Orlowitz David, Ignacio Delgadillo, Virginie De Visscher, Sara Dolnicar, Aldyn Donnelly, Kieran Findlater, Tim Hasid, Jordi Honey-Rosés, Ryan Johnson, Jesse Keenan, Otho Kerr, Rainer Lempert, Helene Loberg, Gloria Loree, Annie Lowrey, Megana Madhurakavi, Allen McConnell, Davis Meyer, Lorien Nesbitt, Anthony Ong, Lars Petersen, Will Porter, Michael Preysman, Michael Prinzing, Amina Razvi, Aaron Sachs, Leslie Samuelrich, Victoria Savalei, Konark Saxena, Rusty and Julie Silverstein, Ya-Yen Sun, Natalie Thivierge, Frans Tjallingii, Myha Truong-Regan, and George Ward.

We wrote most of this book at two coffee shops: Matchstick Yaletown and Kits Beach Coffee. We are grateful to the staff for giving us warm smiles and hot coffee, day in and day out.

Our academic research on happiness and climate action has been led by our stellar graduate student Jade Radke and supported by the Social Sciences and Humanities Research Council (SSHRC). We are so grateful for Canada's continued commitment to supporting climate and behavioral science research. Thank you, Canada!

NOTES

CHAPTER 1. Happiness Is Our Best Weapon

1. Caroline Hickman et al., "Climate Anxiety in Children and Young People and Their Beliefs About Government Responses to Climate Change: A Global Survey," *Lancet Planetary Health* 5, no. 12 (2021): e863–73, https://doi.org/10.1016/S2542-5196(21)00278-3.

2. Michael Prinzing, "Proenvironmental Behavior Increases Subjective Well-Being: Evidence from an Experience-Sampling Study and a Randomized Experiment," *Psychological Science* 35, no. 9 (2024): 951–61, https://doi.org/10.1177/09567976241251766.

3. Michael Prinzing et al., "Pro-Environmental Behaviors and Well-Being in Everyday Life," *Journal of Environmental Psychology* 98 (September 2024): 102394, https://doi.org/10.1016/j.jenvp.2024.102394.

4. Matthew Ballew et al., "Is Distress About Climate Change Associated with Climate Action?" Yale Program on Climate Change Communication, August 3, 2023, https://climatecommunication.yale.edu/publications/distress-about-climate-change-and-climate-action.

5. Matthew O'Brien, "No, Sex Won't Make You Rich," *Atlantic*, August 21, 2013, https://www.theatlantic.com/business/archive/2013/08/no-sex -wont-make-you-rich/278818.

6. Madalina Vlasceanu et al., "Addressing Climate Change with Behavioral Science: A Global Intervention Tournament in 63 Countries," *Science Advances* 10, no. 6 (2024): eadj5778, https://doi.org/10.1126/sciadv .adj5778.

7. Alice M. Isen et al., "Positive Affect Facilitates Creative Problem Solving," *Journal of Personality and Social Psychology* 52, no. 6 (1987): 1122–31, https://doi.org/10.1037/0022-3514.52.6.1122.

8. Patrick Flavin and Michael J. Keane, "Life Satisfaction and Political Participation: Evidence from the United States," *Journal of Happiness Studies* 13 (March 2012): 63–78, https://doi.org/10.1007/s10902-011 -9250-1.

9. Yang Zhong and Jie Chen, "To Vote or Not to Vote: An Analysis of Peasants' Participation in Chinese Village Elections," *Comparative Political Studies* 35, no. 6 (2002): 686–712, https://doi.org/10.1177/001041 4002035006003.

10. Barbara L. Fredrickson et al., "The Undoing Effect of Positive Emotions," *Motivation and Emotion* 24, no. 4 (2000): 237–58, https://doi .org/10.1023/a:1010796329158.

11. Anirudh Tiwathia et al., "And Just Like That: Small Moments on Screen Can Boost Climate-Friendly Food Norms," Rare, August 1, 2024, https://rare.org/research-reports/and-just-like-that-small-moments-on -screen-can-boost-climate-friendly-food-norms.

12. Rachit Dubey et al., "AI-Generated Visuals of Car-Free US Cities Help Improve Support for Sustainable Policies," *Nature Sustainability* 7, no. 4 (2024): 399–403, https://doi.org/10.1038/s41893-024-01299-6.

13. Judy Woodruff, "Dr. Collins Reflects on Career at NIH, COVID Response Effort, Work on Genome Sequencing," PBS News, December 20, 2021, https:// www.pbs.org/newshour/show/dr-collins

-reflects-on-career-at-nih-covid-response-effort-work-on-genome
-sequencing.

14. Felix Creutzig et al., "Demand, Services and Social Aspects of Mitigation," in *Climate Change 2022: Mitigation of Climate Change*, ed. Intergovernmental Panel on Climate Change (Cambridge University Press, 2022), https://doi.org/10.1017/9781009157926.007.

15. Seth Wynes et al., "How Well Do People Understand the Climate Impact of Individual Actions?" *Climatic Change* 162, no. 3 (2020): 1521–34, https://doi.org/10.1007/s10584-020-02811-5.

16. Petteri Taalas, foreword to *IPCC Special Report on Global Warming of 1.5°C* (Intergovernmental Panel on Climate Change, 2018), https://www.ipcc.ch/sr15/about/foreword.

17. Lucas Chancel, "Global Carbon Inequality over 1990–2019," *Nature Sustainability* 5, no. 11 (2022): 931–8, https://doi.org/10.1038/s41893-022-00955-z.

18. Ricardo Gomez-Carrera et al., *Global Inequality Update 2024: New Insights from Extended WID Macro Series* (World Inequality Lab, 2024), https://wid.world/document/global-inequality-update-2024-technical-note.

CHAPTER 2. In Defense of Bacon

1. Diana Ivanova et al., "Quantifying the Potential for Climate Change Mitigation of Consumption Options," *Environmental Research Letters* 15, no. 9 (2020): 093001, https://doi.org/10.1088/1748-9326/ab8589.

2. "Study of Current and Former Vegetarians and Vegans," Faunalytics, December 22, 2014, https://faunalytics.org/study-of-current-and-former-vegetarians-and-vegans.

3. "Jon Stewart: Going Vegan Is the Solution to So Many of the World's Problems," *EcoWatch*, April 7, 2015, https://www.ecowatch.com/jon

-stewart-going-vegan-is-the-solution-to-so-many-of-the-worlds-probl
-1882026750.html.

4. Claire Valentine, "Waka Flocka Flame on Bitcoin, Gucci Mane and Why Vegans Are like Cops," *Paper*, January 17, 2018, https://www.pa permag.com/waka-flocka-flame.

5. Jeffrey M. Jones, "In U.S., 4% Identify as Vegetarian, 1% as Vegan," Gallup, August 24, 2023, https://news.gallup.com/poll/510038/identify -vegetarian-vegan.aspx.

6. "Veganism by Country 2024," World Population Review, https://world populationreview.com/country-rankings/veganism-by-country.

7. Joseph Poore and Thomas Nemecek, "Reducing Food's Environmental Impacts Through Producers and Consumers," *Science* 360, no. 6392 (2018): 987–92, https://doi.org/10.1126/science.aaq0216.

8. "Pork Is the Other White Meat," Best Stop Supermarket, September 28, 2020, https://www.beststopinscott.com/how-pork-became-the-other -white-meat.

9. Tim Emmott, "When It Comes to Sustainability, Not All Nuts Are Created Equal," Nutcellars, October 2, 2020, https://www.nutcellars .com/blog/sustainability-not-all-nuts-are-created-equal.

10. Poore and Nemecek, "Reducing Food's Environmental Impacts."

11. "Environmental Benefits," Maple from Canada, January 30, 2019, https://www.maplefromcanada.com/about/environmental-benefits.

12. Chloe Berge, "The Foods That Reverse Climate Change," BBC, https:// www.bbc.com/future/bespoke/follow-the-food/the-foods-that-reverse -climate-change.

13. Y. Luo and Jiaying Zhao, "Climate-Friendly Food Label Pilot at UBC Open Kitchen," working paper (University of British Columbia, 2022).

14. Paul M. Lohmann et al., "Do Carbon Footprint Labels Promote Clima-tarian Diets? Evidence from a Large-Scale Field Experiment," *Journal of*

Environmental Economics and Management 114 (July 2022): 102693, https://doi.org/10.1016/j.jeem.2022.102693.

15. Bonnie Vockeroth, "Climate-Friendly Food Labels Are Making Sustainable Food Choices Easier on Campus," Food at UBC Vancouver, https://food.ubc.ca/climate-friendly-food-labels.

16. "Jon Stewart: Going Vegan."

17. Hidaya Aliouche, "Impact of Chocolate on Our Climate," News-Medical, September 27, 2021, https://www.news-medical.net/health/Impact-of-Chocolate-on-our-Climate.aspx.

18. Shane Frederick and George Loewenstein, "Hedonic Adaptation," in *Well-Being: Foundations of Hedonic Psychology*, ed. Daniel Kahneman et al. (Russell Sage Foundation, 1999), 302–29.

19. Richard E. Lucas et al., "Reexamining Adaptation and the Set Point Model of Happiness: Reactions to Changes in Marital Status," *Journal of Personality and Social Psychology* 84, no. 3 (2003): 527–39, https://doi.org/10.1037/0022-3514.84.3.527.

20. Jordi Quoidbach and Elizabeth W. Dunn, "Give It Up: A Strategy for Combating Hedonic Adaptation," *Social Psychological and Personality Science* 4, no. 5 (2013): 563–68, https://doi.org/10.1177/1948550612473489.

21. Beyoncé (@Beyonce), "My Greenprint Is," Instagram post, January 30, 2019, https://www.instagram.com/beyonce/p/BtSNVwqAmXv/?img_index=2, and Sabrina Barr, "Beyoncé Announces Vegan Diet in Preparation for Coachella," *Independent*, March 5, 2018, https://www.independent.co.uk/life-style/food-and-drink/beyonce-vegan-coachella-festival-headlining-instagram-nutrition-meal-planner-a8240231.html.

22. Björn Ólafsson, "Meat Consumption Is Rising—but Not in the Way You Think," Sentient Climate, November 15, 2023, https://sentientmedia.org/meat-consumption-rising-not-the-way-you-think.

23. Dinner Menu, Ruth's Chris Steak House, https://ruthschris.com/dallas/fine-dining/dinner-menu.

24. Yann Cornil and Pierre Chandon, "Pleasure as a Substitute for Size: How Multisensory Imagery Can Make People Happier with Smaller Food Portions," *Journal of Marketing Research* 53, no. 5 (2016): 847–64, https://doi.org/10.1509/jmr.14.0299.

25. Camille Schwartz et al., "Effects of Snack Portion Size on Anticipated and Experienced Hunger, Eating Enjoyment, and Perceived Healthiness Among Children," *International Journal of Behavioral Nutrition and Physical Activity* 17, no. 1 (2020), https://doi.org/10.1186/s12966-020-00974-z.

26. Barbara J. Rolls et al., "Sensory Specific Satiety in Man," *Physiology & Behavior* 27, no. 1 (1981): 137–42, https://doi.org/10.1016/0031-9384 (81)90310-3.

27. Edmund T. Rolls et al., "Hunger Modulates the Responses to Gustatory Stimuli of Single Neurons in the Caudolateral Orbitofrontal Cortex of the Macaque Monkey," *European Journal of Neuroscience* 1, no. 1 (1989): 53–60, https://doi.org/10.1111/j.1460-9568.1989.tb00774.x.

28. Michael Pollan, *Food Rules: An Eater's Manual* (Penguin, 2009), 111.

29. Cornil and Chandon, "Pleasure as a Substitute for Size."

30. Pierre Chandon and Yann Cornil, "More Value from Less Food? Effects of Epicurean Labeling on Moderate Eating in the United States and in France," *Appetite* 178 (November 2022): 106262, https://doi.org/10.1016/j.appet.2022.106262.

31. P. Rozin et al., "Attitudes to Food and the Role of Food in Life in the U.S.A., Japan, Flemish Belgium and France: Possible Implications for the Diet–Health Debate," *Appetite* 33, no. 2 (1999): 163–80, https://doi.org/10.1006/appe.1999.0244.

32. Yann Cornil and Pierre Chandon, "Pleasure as an Ally of Healthy Eating? Contrasting Visceral and Epicurean Eating Pleasure and Their Association with Portion Size Preferences and Wellbeing," *Appetite* 104 (September 2016): 52–9, https://doi.org/10.1016/j.appet.2015.08.045.

33. Chandon and Cornil, "More Value from Less Food?"

34. David G. Blanchflower et al., "Is Psychological Well-Being Linked to the Consumption of Fruit and Vegetables?" *Social Indicators Research* 114, no. 3 (2013): 785–801, https://doi.org/10.1007/s11205-012 -0173-y.

35. Neel Ocean et al., "Lettuce Be Happy: The Effects of Fruit and Vegetable Consumption on Subjective Well-Being in the UK," *SSRN Electronic Journal* (July 2018), https://doi.org/10.2139/ssrn.3211798.

36. Redzo Mujcic and Andrew J. Oswald, "Evolution of Well-Being and Happiness After Increases in Consumption of Fruit and Vegetables," *American Journal of Public Health* 106, no. 8 (2016): 1504–10, https://doi .org/10.2105/ajph.2016.303260.

37. Angela De Leon et al., "Consumption of Dietary Guidelines for Americans Types and Amounts of Vegetables Increases Mean Subjective Happiness Scale Scores: A Randomized Controlled Trial," *Journal of the Academy of Nutrition and Dietetics* 122, no. 7 (2022): 1355–62, https://doi .org/10.1016/j.jand.2021.11.009.

38. Tamlin S. Conner et al., "Let Them Eat Fruit! The Effect of Fruit and Vegetable Consumption on Psychological Well-Being in Young Adults: A Randomized Controlled Trial," *PloS One* 12, no. 2 (2017): e0171206, htts://doi.org/10.1371/journal.pone.0171206.

39. "22 Days Nutrition," YouTube video, 4:26, posted by Beyoncé, June 10, 2015, https://www.youtube.com/watch?v=0GKqil3a7po.

40. Leif D. Nelson et al., "Psychology's Renaissance," *Annual Review of Psychology* 69, no. 1 (2018): 511–34, https://doi.org/10.1146/annurev -psych-122216-011836.

41. Kathryn Asher et al., "Study of Current and Former Vegetarians and Vegans" (Humane Research Council, December 2014), https://faunalytics .org/wp-content/uploads/2015/06/Faunalytics_Current-Former -Vegetarians_Full-Report.pdf.

42. Toshiyuki Nakagaki et al., "Maze-Solving by an Amoeboid Organism," *Nature* 407, no. 6803 (2000): 470, https://doi.org/10.1038/35035159.

43. Atsushi Tero et al., "Rules for Biologically Inspired Adaptive Network Design," *Science* 327, no. 5964 (2010): 439–42, https://doi.org/10.1126/science.1177894.

44. Quantis, "Comparative Life Cycle Assessment of Meals from Hello-Fresh Meal Kits, Restaurant Delivery and Supermarket," HelloFresh, May 2022, https://cdn.hellofresh.com/de/cms/HelloFresh_Meal_Kit_Life_Cycle_Assessment_Study.pdf.

45. Apicius, *Cooking and Dining in Imperial Rome*, trans. J. D. Vehling (Springer, 1936).

46. Ellen van Kleef et al., "Nudging Children Towards Whole Wheat Bread: A Field Experiment on the Influence of Fun Bread Roll Shape on Breakfast Consumption," *BMC Public Health* 14, no. 1 (2014), https://doi.org/10.1186/1471-2458-14-906.

47. Alain D. Starke et al., "Nudging Healthy Choices in Food Search Through Visual Attractiveness," *Frontiers in Artificial Intelligence* 4 (2021): 621743, https://doi.org/10.3389/frai.2021.621743.

48. Rose M. Pangborn et al., "The Influence of Color on Discrimination of Sweetness in Dry Table-Wine," *American Journal of Psychology* 76, no. 3 (1963): 492–5, https://doi.org/10.2307/1419795.

49. Charles Spence, "On the Relationship(s) Between Color and Taste/Flavor," *Experimental Psychology* 66, no. 2 (2019): 99–111, https://doi.org/10.1027/1618-3169/a000439.

50. Carmen E. Lefevre and David I. Perrett, "Fruit over Sunbed: Carotenoid Skin Colouration Is Found More Attractive Than Melanin Colouration," *Quarterly Journal of Experimental Psychology* 68, no. 2 (2015): 284–93, https://doi.org/10.1080/17470218.2014.944194.

51. Chelsea D. Christie and Frances S. Chen, "Vegetarian or Meat? Food Choice Modeling of Main Dishes Occurs Outside of Awareness," *Appetite* 121 (February 2018): 50–4, https://doi.org/10.1016/j.appet.2017.10.036.

52. Kristina Gligorić et al., "Formation of Social Ties Influences Food Choice: A Campus-Wide Longitudinal Study," *Proceedings of the ACM on Human-Computer Interaction* 5, no. CSCW1 (2021): 1–25.

53. Giada Danesi, "Pleasures and Stress of Eating Alone and Eating Together Among French and German Young Adults," *Menu: The Journal of Eating and Hospitality Research* 1 (2012): 77–91.

54. David Whitney and Dennis M. Levi, "Visual Crowding: A Fundamental Limit on Conscious Perception and Object Recognition," *Trends in Cognitive Sciences* 15, no. 4 (2011): 160–8, https://doi.org/10.1016/j .tics.2011.02.005.

55. Jane Dai et al., "Perceptual Salience Influences Food Choices Independently of Health and Taste Preferences," *Cognitive Research: Principles and Implications* 5, no. 1 (2020): 1–13, https://doi.org/10.1186/s41235 -019-0203-2.

56. Christina Gravert and Verena Kurz, "Nudging à la Carte: A Field Experiment on Climate-Friendly Food Choice," *Behavioural Public Policy* 5, no. 3 (2021): 378–95, https://doi.org/10.1017/bpp.2019.11.

57. "Americans Waste Nearly a Pound of Food Each per Day, Study Finds," CBS News, April 18, 2018, https://www.cbsnews.com/news/americans -waste-nearly-a-pound-of-food-each-per-day-study-finds.

58. "From Farm to Kitchen: The Environmental Impacts of U.S. Food Waste," United States Environmental Protection Agency, November 17, 2021, https://www.epa.gov/land-research/farm-kitchen-environmental -impacts-us-food-waste.

59. "Importance of Methane," United States Environmental Protection Agency, January 11, 2016, https://www.epa.gov/gmi/importance -methane.

60. Annie Lalande et al., "Planetary Health Menu Study at VGH," working paper (University of British Columbia, 2025).

CHAPTER 3. How to Buy Low-Carbon Happiness

1. Kyla Hunter, "A Toonie Party," *Where Is the World?* (blog), November 12, 2015, https://www.whereistheworld.ca/a-toonie-party.

2. Valentina Bisinella et al., *Life Cycle Assessment of Grocery Carrier Bags*, Ministry of Environment and Food of Denmark (Danish Environmental Protection Agency, 2018), https://www2.mst.dk/udgiv/publications /2018/02/978-87-93614-73-4.pdf.

3. Angela D. La Rosa and Sotirios A. Grammatikos, "Comparative Life Cycle Assessment of Cotton and Other Natural Fibers for Textile Applications," *Fibers* 7, no. 12 (2019): 101, https://doi.org/10.3390 /fib7120101.

4. Hannah Ritchie, "Is Organic Really Better for the Environment Than Conventional Agriculture?" Our World in Data, October 19, 2017, https://ourworldindata.org/is-organic-agriculture-better-for-the -environment.

5. Pauline Boisacq et al., "Assessment of Poly- and Perfluoroalkyl Substances (PFAS) in Commercially Available Drinking Straws Using Targeted and Suspect Screening Approaches," *Food Additives & Contaminants: Part A* 40, no. 9 (2023), https://www.tandfonline.com /doi/abs/10.1080/19440049.2023.2240908.

6. Huier Chen et al., "Release of Microplastics from Disposable Cups in Daily Use," *Science of the Total Environment* 854 (January 2023): 158606, https://doi.org/10.1016/j.scitotenv.2022.158606.

7. David Evans, "Reusable vs Single-Use Water Bottles: What's Better for the Environment?" Plastic Education, December 7, 2023, https://plastic .education/reusable-vs-single-use-water-bottles-whats-better-for-the -environment.

8. Sadegh Shahmohammadi et al., "Comparative Greenhouse Gas Footprinting of Online Versus Traditional Shopping for Fast-Moving Consumer Goods: A Stochastic Approach," *Environmental Science &*

Technology 54, no. 6 (2020): 3499–3509, https://doi.org/10.1021/acs
.est.9b06252.

9. Daniel Kahneman et al., "A Survey Method for Characterizing Daily Life Experience: The Day Reconstruction Method," *Science* 306, no. 5702 (2004): 1776–80, https://doi.org/10.1126/science.1103572.

10. Hannah Ritchie, "Very Little of Global Food Is Transported by Air; This Greatly Reduces the Climate Benefits of Eating Local," Our World in Data, January 28, 2020, https://ourworldindata.org/food-transport-by-mode.

11. "The Climate Footprint Across the IKEA Value Chain," IKEA, https://www.ikea.com/global/en/our-business/sustainability/value-chain-climate-footprint.

12. "Consumers Willing to Pay 9.7% Sustainability Premium, Even as Cost-of-Living and Inflationary Concerns Weigh: PwC 2024 Voice of the Consumer Survey," PricewaterhouseCoopers press release, May 15, 2024, https://www.pwc.com/gx/en/news-room/press-releases/2024/pwc-2024-voice-of-consumer-survey.html.

13. Béatrice Parguel et al., "Can Evoking Nature in Advertising Mislead Consumers? The Power of 'Executional Greenwashing,'" *International Journal of Advertising* 34, no 1 (2015): 107–34, https://www.tandfonline.com/doi/abs/10.1080/02650487.2014.996116.

14. Rashmila Maiti, "The Environmental Impact of Fast Fashion, Explained," Earth.org, January 20, 2025, https://earth.org/fast-fashions-detrimental-effect-on-the-environment.

15. *The Life Cycle of a Jean* (Levi Strauss & Co., 2015), https://www.levistrauss.com/wp-content/uploads/2015/03/Full-LCA-Results-Deck-FINAL.pdf.

16. G. Peters et. al., "Carbon Footprints in the Textile Industry," in *Handbook of Life Cycle Assessment (LCA) of Textiles and Clothing*, ed. Subramanian Senthilkannan Muthu (Woodhead, 2015), 3–30, https://doi.org/10.1016/B978-0-08-100169-1.00001-0.

17. Peters et al., "Carbon Footprints."

18. Esteban Ortiz-Ospina et al., "Time Use," Our World in Data, February 2024, https://ourworldindata.org/time-use.

19. Luciano Rodrigues Viana et al., "Would Transitioning from Conventional to Organic Oat Grains Production Reduce Environmental Impacts? A LCA Case Study in North-East Canada," *Journal of Cleaner Production* 349 (May 2022), https://doi.org/10.1016/j.jclepro.2022.131344.

20. Frederic J. Frommer, "Jimmy Carter Wore a Sweater—and Ignited Years of Republican Backlash," *Washington Post*, October 1, 2024, https://www.washingtonpost.com/history/2024/10/01/jimmy-carter-sweater-environment.

21. Frommer, "Jimmy Carter Wore a Sweater."

22. Seth Wynes et al., "How Well Do People Understand the Climate Impact of Individual Actions?" *Climatic Change* 162 (August 2020): 1521–34, https://doi.org/10.1007/s10584-020-02811-5.

23. Diana Ivanova et al., "Quantifying the Potential for Climate Change Mitigation of Consumption Options," *Environmental Research Letters* 15, no. 9 (2020), https://doi.org/10.1088/1748-9326/ab8589.

24. Shigehiro Oishi et al., "Income Inequality and Happiness," *Psychological Science* 22, no. 9 (2011): 1095–100, https://doi.org/10.1177/0956797611417262.

25. Gillian M. Sandstrom and Elizabeth W. Dunn, "Social Interactions and Well-Being: The Surprising Power of Weak Ties," *Personality and Social Psychology Bulletin* 40, no. 7 (2014): 910–22, https://doi.org/10.1177/0146167214529799.

26. Kristina Shampanier et al., "Zero as a Special Price: The True Value of Free Products," *Marketing Science* 26, no. 6 (2007): 742–57, https://doi.org/10.1287/mksc.1060.0254.

27. Dan Ariely et al., "Social Norms and the Price of Zero," *Journal of Consumer Psychology* 28, no. 2 (2018): 180–91, https://doi.org/10.1002/jcpy.1018.

28. Jamie Beck Alexander et al., "Saving (for) the Planet: The Climate Power of Personal Banking," Project Drawdown, December 2023, https://draw down.org/publications/saving-for-the-planet.

29. Neil Simpson, "How to Stop Funding Fossil Fuels by Moving to an Ethical Bank," *Extinction Rebellion* (blog), September 21, 2020, https:// rebellion.global/blog/2020/09/21/ethical-banks.

30. "Help Shape the Future of 401(k)s," https://cdn.prod.website-files.com /6310f9983f7764c4dbfe70eb/63348502cda69482e3519713_62325ca9 7b0fd067573e3730_survey2021.pdf.

31. Matthew A. Killingsworth et al., "Income and Emotional Well-Being: A Conflict Resolved," *Proceedings of the National Academy of Sciences* 120, no. 10 (2023): e2208661120, https://doi.org/10.1073/pnas.2208661120.

32. "Climate Action Plan," Costco Wholesale, December 2024, https://mo bilecontent.costco.com/staging/resource/img/25w03130/5a_Climate ActionPlan_FY24.pdf.

33. "Release: Green Century Shareholder Proposal Prompts Costco Commitment to Set New Climate Emissions Reduction Targets," news release, November 16, 2022, https://www.greencentury.com/release-green -century-shareholder-proposal-prompts-costco-commitment-to-set-new -climate-emissions-reduction-targets.

34. "The Mystery Experiment," TED, https://www.ted.com/about/pro grams-initiatives/the-mystery-experiment.

35. Säde Stenlund et al., "How Spending Decisions Shape Happiness in Everyday Life," *Communications Psychology*, 2, no 124 (2024): 1-6, https:// doi.org/10.1038/s44271-024-00166-6.

36. "The Green Streets Program: Volunteer Gardening on Traffic Calming Spaces," City of Vancouver, https://vancouver.ca/home-property -development/green-streets-program.aspx.

CHAPTER 4. The Odyssey of Rush Hour

1. Jordi Honey-Rosés, "The Global Bike Bus Movement," City Lab Barcelona, January 9, 2024, https://citylabbcn.org/the-global-bike-bus-movement.

2. Arthur A. Stone and Stefan Schneider, "Commuting Episodes in the United States: Their Correlates with Experiential Wellbeing from the American Time Use Survey," *Transportation Research Part F: Traffic Psychology and Behaviour* 42 (October 2016): 117–24, https://doi.org/10.1016/j.trf.2016.07.004.

3. Margo Hilbrecht et al., "Highway to Health? Commute Time and Well-Being Among Canadian Adults," *World Leisure Journal* 56, no. 2 (2014): 151–63, https://doi.org/https://doi.org/10.1080/16078055.2014.903723.

4. Erika Sandow, "Til Work Do Us Part: The Social Fallacy of Long-Distance Commuting," *Urban Studies* 51, no. 3 (2013): 526–43, https://doi.org/10.1177/0042098013498280.

5. RaShawn Mitchner, "Daily Drives: U.S. Commute Trends," MarketWatch Guides, August 21, 2024, https://www.marketwatch.com/guides/insurance-services/us-commute-trends.

6. Kolin Schunck, "2021 Update: Average Carbon Emissions by Transport Type," TNMT, February 15, 2021, https://public.tableau.com/views/UpdateAveragecarbonemissionsbytransportmodebrokendownbycategory2_0TNMT/AVERAGECARBONEMISSIONSBYTRANSPORTMODE?:showVizHome=no.

7. Oliver Smith, "Commute Well-Being Differences by Mode: Evidence from Portland, Oregon, USA," *Journal of Transport & Health* 4 (March 2017): 246–54, https://doi.org/10.1016/j.jth.2016.08.005.

8. Sammi R. Chekroud et al., "Association Between Physical Exercise and Mental Health in 1.2 Million Individuals in the USA Between 2011 and 2015: A Cross-Sectional Study," *Lancet Psychiatry* 5, no. 9 (2018): 739–46, https://doi.org/10.1016/s2215-0366(18)30227-x.

9. Mark Sutton, "Electric Bike Sales Around the World Pass Key Milestones," Cycling Electric, March 17, 2025, https://www.cyclingelectric.com/in-depth/electric-bike-sales-around-the-world-pass-key-milestones.

10. Nancy McGuckin and Anthony Fucci, *Summary of Travel Trends: 2017 National Household Travel Survey* (US Department of Transportation, Federal Highway Administration, 2018), https://nhts.ornl.gov/assets/2017_nhts_summary_travel_trends.pdf.

11. "NJ Students Commuting to School on 'Bike Bus,'" YouTube video, 2:55, posted by FOX 5 New York, June 16, 2023, https://www.youtube.com/watch?v=-pGTt9Yyi8o.

12. "Hudson River Greenway," TrailLink, https://www.traillink.com/trail/hudson-river-greenway.

13. Henry Mance, "Paris Mayor Anne Hidalgo: 'A City's Creativity Doesn't Depend on Cars. That's the 20th Century,'" *Financial Times*, March 12, 2023, https://www.ft.com/content/8fbad76c-6705-43d8-b57e-292ee3563539.

14. Iwona Alfred and Alphonse Tam, "2023 STA Winner Paris, France Presents a Bold Vision for Its Historic Streets," Institute for Transportation and Development Policy, April 2, 2024, https://itdp.org/2024/04/02/2023-sta-paris-france-presents-a-bold-vision-for-historic-streets.

15. "City Ratings: Minneapolis Minnesota, United States," PeopleForBikes, https://cityratings.peopleforbikes.org/cities/minneapolis-mn.

16. Sarah Ryals, "What If Your Morning Commute Was Designed for Joy?" Streets.mn, September 22, 2022, https://streets.mn/2022/09/22/commute-designed-for-joy.

17. Alberto Castro et al., "Physical Activity of Electric Bicycle Users Compared to Conventional Bicycle Users and Non-Cyclists: Insights Based on Health and Transport Data from an Online Survey in Seven European Cities," *Transportation Research Interdisciplinary Perspectives* 1 (June 2019): 100017, https://doi.org/10.1016/j.trip.2019.100017.

18. Carolina Muguruza et al., "The Motivation for Exercise over Palatable Food Is Dictated by Cannabinoid Type-1 Receptors," *JCI Insight* 4, no. 5 (2019), https://doi.org/10.1172/jci.insight.126190.

19. Hannah Steinberg et al., "Exercise Enhances Creativity Independently of Mood," *British Journal of Sports Medicine* 31, no. 3 (1997): 240–5, https://doi.org/10.1136/bjsm.31.3.240.

20. Wenyi Zhang, "High-Speed Railway in China—Statistics & Facts," Statista, May 7, 2024, https://www.statista.com/topics/7534/high-speed -rail-in-china.

21. Fanglin Chen and Zhongfei Chen, "High-Speed Rail and Happiness," *Transportation Research Part A: Policy and Practice* 170 (April 2023): 103635, https://doi.org/10.1016/j.tra.2023.103635.

22. Wan Li et al., "Does Metro Proximity Promote Happiness? Evidence from Shanghai," *Journal of Transport and Land Use* 11, no. 1 (2018), https://doi.org/10.5198/jtlu.2018.1286.

23. Guillaume Rivard, "Study: Most Cars Are Left Unused 95 Percent of the Year," Car Guide, January 19, 2022, https://www.guideautoweb.com /en/articles/64149/etude-la-majorite-des-voitures-restent-inutilisees -95-pc-du-temps.

24. Uber + BIT, *One Less Car: Exploring Barriers and Opportunities for a Car-Light Future in the US and Canada*, https://uber.app.box.com/s/3jk 1u387p9q38jp4phmvaxdkg9buemp7.

25. "Uber's Electrification Update," Uber, https://www.uber.com/us/en /about/reports/sustainability-report.

26. "Millions of Trips a Day, Zero Emissions and a Shift to Sustainable Packaging," Uber, https://www.uber.com/us/en/about/sustainability.

27. "Go Electric to Maximize Your Earnings," Lyft, https://www.lyft.com /driver/go-electric.

28. *Sustainability Report 2023* (Lime Technologies, 2023), https://investors .lime-technologies.com/wp-content/uploads/2024/04/Lime -Sustainability-Report-2023.pdf.

29. Stephanie Sierra and Lindsey Feingold, "CA Roads Are 3rd Deadliest in US for Pedestrians, Data Shows. Here's How Bay Area Counties Fare," ABC7 News, January 25, 2024, https://abc7news.com/pedestrian -deaths-california-fatalities-accident-data-traffic-cameras/14357193.

30. "Past the Limit: Studying How Often Drivers Speed in San Francisco and Phoenix," *Waypoint* (blog), July 11, 2023, https://waymo.com/blog /2023/07/past-the-limit-studying-how-often-drivers-speed-in-san -francisco-and-phoenix.

31. Adam Forrest, "'We've Become Good Friends': Carpooling Eases Drudgery of Commuting," *Guardian*, April 26, 2017, https://www.the guardian.com/sustainable-business/2017/apr/26/carpooling-commuting -car-share-liftshare-uber.

32. Sascha Lancée et al., "Commuting and Happiness: What Ways Feel Best for What Kinds of People?" In *Quality of Life and Daily Travel*, ed. Margareta Friman et al. (Springer, 2018), 73–93, https://link.springer .com/chapter/10.1007/978-3-319-76623-2_5.

33. Mike Murphy, "I Sing (and Whine) the Car Electric," *Mike Murphy's Barking at the Moon Blabfest* (Substack), September 6, 2023, https://mi chael96.substack.com/p/i-sing-and-whine-the-car-electric.

34. Charles Morris, "EVs Are for Everybody—but How to Get Republicans to Buy Them?" *Charged*, February 15, 2024, https://chargedevs.com /newswire/evs-are-for-everybody-but-how-to-get-republicans-to-buy -them.

35. "How Norway Built an EV Utopia While the U.S. Is Struggling to Go Electric | CNBC Documentary," YouTube video, 36:41, posted by CNBC, February 17, 2024, https://www.youtube.com/watch?v=R5D bRyeZNRk.

36. Karin Kirk, "Electric Vehicles Reduce Carbon Pollution in All U.S. States," *Yale Climate Connections*, September 14, 2023, https://yalecli mateconnections.org/2023/09/electric-vehicles-reduce-carbon -pollution-in-all-u-s-states.

37. Lakshmi R B, "The Environmental Impact of Battery Production for Electric Vehicles," Earth.org, January 11, 2023, https://earth.org/environmental-impact-of-battery-production.

38. Laura Roberson et al., "Battery-Powered Bargains? Assessing Electric Vehicle Resale Value in the United States," *Environmental Research Letters* 19, no. 5 (2024): 054053, https://doi.org/10.1088/1748-9326/ad3fce.

39. Xiaoning Xia et al., "Life Cycle Carbon Footprint of Electric Vehicles in Different Countries: A Review," *Separation and Purification Technology* 301 (November 2022): 122063, https://doi.org/10.1016/j.seppur.2022.122063.

40. Diana Ivanova et al., "Quantifying the Potential for Climate Change Mitigation of Consumption Options," *Environmental Research Letters* 15, no. 9 (2020), https://doi.org/10.1088/1748-9326/ab8589.

41. "Boosting Health for Children: Benefits of Zero-Emission Transportation and Electricity," American Lung Association, February 2024, https://www.lung.org/getmedia/dec4362b-0467-4609-9639-2e62301409a4/EV-Boosting-Health-for-Children.pdf.

42. Maximilian Holland, "EVs Take 97.4% Share in Norway—Tesla Model Y Best Seller," CleanTechnica, May 11, 2025, https://cleantechnica.com/2025/05/09/evs-take-97-4-share-in-norway.

43. Ivanova et al., "Quantifying the Potential."

44. Yanqiu Tao et al., "Climate Mitigation Potentials of Teleworking Are Sensitive to Changes in Lifestyle and Workplace Rather than ICT Usage," *Proceedings of the National Academy of Sciences* 120, no. 39 (2023): e2304099120, https://doi.org/10.1073/pnas.2304099120.

45. Jose Maria Barrero et al., "Why Working from Home Will Stick," Working Paper 28731 (National Bureau of Economic Research, 2021), https://www.nber.org/papers/w28731.

Jose Maria Barrero et al., "SWAA July 2024 Updates," WFH Research, July 5, 2024, https://wfhresearch.com/wp-content/uploads/2024/07/WFHResearch_updates_July2024.pdf.

46. Nicholas Bloom et al., "Does Working from Home Work? Evidence from a Chinese Experiment," *Quarterly Journal of Economics* 130, no. 1 (2015): 165–218, https://doi.org/10.1093/qje/qju032.

47. "Go Ahead, Tell Your Boss You Are Working from Home | Nicholas Bloom | TEDxStanford," YouTube video, 14:31, posted by TEDx Talks, May 22, 2017, https://www.youtube.com/watch?v=oiUyyZPIHyY.

48. Natalia Emanuel et al., "The Power of Proximity to Coworkers: Training for Tomorrow or Productivity Today?" Working Paper 31880 (National Bureau of Economic Research, 2023), http://dx.doi.org/10.3386/w31880.

49. Casey Newton, "Mark Zuckerberg on Taking His Massive Workforce Remote," *Verge*, May 21, 2020, https://www.theverge.com/2020/5/21/21265780/facebook-remote-work-mark-zuckerberg-interview-wfh.

50. Yiling Lin et al., "Remote Collaboration Fuses Fewer Breakthrough Ideas," *Nature* 623, no. 7989 (2023): 987–91, https://doi.org/10.1038/s41586-023-06767-1.

51. Barrero et al., "Why Working from Home"; Barrero et al., "SWAA July 2024 Updates."

52. Nicholas Bloom et al., "Hybrid Working from Home Improves Retention Without Damaging Performance," *Nature* 630, no. 8018 (2024): 920–5, https://doi.org/10.1038/s41586-024-07500-2.

53. Prithwiraj Choudhury et al., "Is Hybrid Work the Best of Both Worlds? Evidence from a Field Experiment," Working Paper No. 22-063 (Harvard Business School, 2022), https://doi.org/10.2139/ssrn.4068741.

54. Cevat Giray Aksoy et al., "Time Savings When Working from Home," *AEA Papers and Proceedings* 113 (May 2023): 597–603, https://doi.org/10.1257/pandp.20231013.

55. Elizabeth Linos, "Does Teleworking Work for Organizations? Measuring the Impact of Working from Home on Retention and Performance," working paper (Harvard University, 2015).

56. Melanie S. Brucks and Jonathan Levav, "Virtual Communication Curbs Creative Idea Generation," *Nature* 605, no. 7908 (2022): 108–12, https://doi.org/10.1038/s41586-022-04643-y.

57. Dan Hammond and Pia Lee, *We Not Me*, podcast, episode 93, "The State of Working from Home with Jose Maria Barrero," Transistor, March 22, 2024, https://share.transistor.fm/s/896618fd.

58. Prithwiraj (Raj) Choudhury et al., "Work-from-Anywhere: The Productivity Effects of Geographic Flexibility," *Strategic Management Journal* 42, no. 4 (2021): 655–83, https://doi.org/10.1002/smj.3251.

59. "40-Hour Work Week: Its History and Future," ActiPlans, May 2024, https://www.actiplans.com/blog/40-hour-work-week.

60. Charlie Giattino et al., "Working Hours," Our World in Data, 2020, https://ourworldindata.org/working-hours.

61. Charlotte Lockhart, "Stop the Clock: The Environmental Benefits of a Shorter Working Week," Platform London, May 25, 2021.

62. "Accelerate Your Path to Business Success," 4 Day Week Global, https://www.4dayweek.com/pilot-program.

63. Kyle Lewis et al., *The Results Are In: The UK's Four-Day Week Pilot* (Autonomy, 2023), https://autonomy.work/wp-content/uploads/2023/02/The-results-are-in-The-UKs-four-day-week-pilot.pdf.

64. Author interview with Ben Sommers and Nita Sommers, July 23, 2024.

65. Konstantinos Chalvatzis and Peter L. Ormosi, "The Carbon Impact of Flying to Economics Conferences: Is Flying More Associated with More Citations?" *Journal of Sustainable Tourism* 29, no. 1 (2021): 40–67, https://doi.org/10.1080/09669582.2020.1806858.

CHAPTER 5. Oh, the Places You'll Go

1. Stewart Barr et al., "Times for (Un)Sustainability? Challenges and Opportunities for Developing Behaviour Change Policy. A Case-Study of

Consumers at Home and Away," *Global Environmental Change* 21, no. 4 (2011): 1234–44, https://doi.org/10.1016/j.gloenvcha.2011.07.011.

2. Thomas Gilovich and Iñigo Gallo, "Consumers' Pursuit of Material and Experiential Purchases: A Review," *Consumer Psychology Review* 3, no. 1 (2020): 20–33, https://doi.org/10.1002/arcp.1053.

3. Colin West et al., "Happiness from Treating the Weekend like a Vacation," *Social Psychological and Personality Science* 12, no. 3 (2020): 346–56, https://doi.org/10.1177/1948550620916080.

4. Jeroen Nawijn, "The Holiday Happiness Curve: A Preliminary Investigation into Mood During a Holiday Abroad," *International Journal of Tourism Research* 12, no. 3 (2010): 281–90, https://doi.org/10.1002/jtr.756.

5. Suzanne B. Shu and Ayelet Gneezy, "Procrastination of Enjoyable Experiences," *Journal of Marketing Research* 47, no. 5 (2010): 933–44, https://doi.org/10.1509/jmkr.47.5.933.

6. Shu and Gneezy, "Procrastination of Enjoyable Experiences."

7. West et al., "Happiness from Treating."

8. David B. Yaden et al., "The Overview Effect: Awe and Self-Transcendent Experience in Space Flight," *Psychology of Consciousness: Theory, Research, and Practice* 3, no. 1 (2016): 1–11, https://doi.org/10.1037/cns0000086.

9. Pico Iyer, "Why We Travel," *Pico Iyer Journeys* (blog), March 18, 2000, https://picoiyerjourneys.com/why-we-travel.

10. Jordi Quoidbach et al., "The Price of Abundance: How a Wealth of Experiences Impoverishes Savoring," *Personality and Social Psychology Bulletin* 41, no. 3 (2015): 393–404, https://doi.org/10.1177/0146167214566189.

11. "12 Ways to Travel Sustainably in the New Year," *National Geographic*, January 8, 2021, https://www.nationalgeographic.com/travel/article/how-to-travel-sustainably-in-new-year.

12. "Chris Rock Wants an Airline with No Security | Total Blackout," YouTube video, 2:40, posted by Netflix Is a Joke, January 15, 2021, https://www.youtube.com/watch?v=Re2dzNZaCSg.

13. "Air Travelers in America: Annual Survey," Airlines for America, March 18, 2025, https://www.airlines.org/dataset/air-travelers-in-america-annual-survey.

14. Erma Bombeck, Goodreads, https://www.goodreads.com/quotes/17683-did-you-ever-notice-that-the-first-piece-of-luggage.

15. "Flying Economy in 2024 (Full Length Video)," YouTube video, 1:01, posted by Josiah Schneider, January 19, 2024, https://www.youtube.com/watch?v=dQa70HpK1vQ.

16. "United Seat Maps," SeatGuru, https://www.seatguru.com/airlines/United_Airlines/United_Airlines_Boeing_737-800_C.php.

17. Gunnar Olson, "Is It Cheaper to Fly Nonstop or with a Layover?" Thrifty Traveler, September 2, 2022, https://thriftytraveler.com/news/travel/nonstop-flight-vs-layover.

18. Jiaying Zhao, "How to Feng Shui Your Fridge—and Other Happy Climate Hacks," TED Talk, New York, February 2023, 12:10, https://www.ted.com/talks/jiaying_zhao_how_to_feng_shui_your_fridge_and_other_happy_climate_hacks.

19. C. Peter Herman and Deborah Mack, "Restrained and Unrestrained Eating," *Journal of Personality* 43, no. 4 (1975): 647–60, https://doi.org/10.1111/j.1467-6494.1975.tb00727.x.

20. "Byway: Flight-Free Holidays by Train, Bus and Ferry," Byway, accessed September 12, 2025, https://www.byway.travel/en-US.

21. Amit Kumar et al., "Waiting for Merlot: Anticipatory Consumption of Experiential and Material Purchases," *Psychological Science* 25, no. 10 (2014): 1924–31, https://doi.org/10.1177/0956797614546556.

22. Kumar et al., "Waiting for Merlot."

23. Suzanne Podhaizer, "The Véloroute Gourmande: Canada's Delectable 235km Food Trail," BBC, October 16, 2024, https://www.bbc.com /travel/article/20241015-the-vloroute-gourmande-canadas-delectable -235km-food-trail.

24. "Cruise Ship Amenities: From the Common to the Extraordinary," Cruise Panorama, https://cruise-panorama.com/new-to-cruising/com mon-amenities-and-provisions-on-a-cruise-ship.

25. Travis J. Carter and Thomas Gilovich, "I Am What I Do, Not What I Have: The Differential Centrality of Experiential and Material Purchases to the Self," *Journal of Personality and Social Psychology* 102, no. 6 (2012): 1304–17, https://doi.org/10.1037/a0027407.

26. Emily Rosenzweig and Thomas Gilovich, "Buyer's Remorse or Missed Opportunity? Differential Regrets for Material and Experiential Purchases," *Journal of Personality and Social Psychology* 102, no. 2 (2012): 215–23, https://doi.org/10.1037/a0024999.

27. "Wallow Fire: Cousins Charged over Arizona Wildfire," BBC News, August 24, 2011, https://www.bbc.com/news/world-us-canada -14658489.

28. "Wildfire Causes and Evaluations," U.S. National Park Service, April 15, 2025, https://www.nps.gov/articles/wildfire-causes-and-evaluation .htm.

29. Mingming Cheng et al., "The Sharing Economy and Sustainability— Assessing Airbnb's Direct, Indirect and Induced Carbon Footprint in Sydney," *Journal of Sustainable Tourism* 28, no. 8 (2020): 1083–99, https:// doi.org/10.1080/09669582.2020.1720698.

30. Dunigan Folk and Elizabeth W. Dunn, "Everything Is Better Together," under review.

31. Raphael Calel et al., "Do Carbon Offsets Offset Carbon?" *American Economic Journal: Applied Economics* 17, no. 1 (2025): 1–40, https://doi .org/10.1257/app.20230052.

32. Katie Lebling et al., "6 Things to Know About Direct Air Capture," World Resources Institute, September 2, 2025, https://www.wri.org/insights/direct-air-capture-resource-considerations-and-costs-carbon-removal.

33. Michael Köhl et al., "The Impact of Tree Age on Biomass Growth and Carbon Accumulation Capacity: A Retrospective Analysis Using Tree Ring Data of Three Tropical Tree Species Grown in Natural Forests of Suriname," *PLoS One* 12, no. 8 (2017): e0181187, https://doi.org/10.1371/journal.pone.0181187.

34. "Efficient and Clean Cooking for Households in Nigeria," Gold Standard, https://marketplace.goldstandard.org/products/key-carbon-limited-efficient-and-clean-cooking-for-households-in-nigeria.

35. Dilip Soman and Amar Cheema, "Earmarking and Partitioning: Increasing Saving by Low-Income Households," *Journal of Marketing Research* 48 (2011): S14–22, https://doi.org/10.1509/jmkr.48.SPL.S14.

CHAPTER 6. Life's Biggest Decisions

1. Cassie Flynn et al., *People's Climate Vote 2024: Results* (United Nations Development Programme, 2024), https://peoplesclimate.vote/document/Peoples_Climate_Vote_Report_2024.pdf.

2. Mona Chalabi, "How Many Times Does the Average Person Move?" FiveThirtyEight, January 29, 2015, https://fivethirtyeight.com/features/how-many-times-the-average-person-moves.

3. Anna Rhodes and Max Besbris, *Soaking the Middle Class: Suburban Inequality and Recovery from Disaster* (Russell Sage Foundation, 2022), https://doi.org/10.7758/9781610449168.

4. John F. Helliwell et al., eds., *World Happiness Report 2024* (University of Oxford: Wellbeing Research Centre, 2024), https://www.worldhappiness.report/ed/2024.

5. David Maddison and Katrin Rehdanz, "The Impact of Climate on Life Satisfaction," *Ecological Economics* 70, no. 12 (2011): 2437–45, https://doi.org/10.1016/j.ecolecon.2011.07.027.

6. Christian Krekel and George MacKerron, "How Environmental Quality Affects Our Happiness," in *World Happiness Report 2020* (Sustainable Development Solutions Network, 2020), https://worldhappiness.report/ed/2020/how-environmental-quality-affects-our-happiness.

7. Chi Xu et al., "Future of the Human Climate Niche," *Proceedings of the National Academy of Sciences* 117, no. 21 (2020): 11350–5, https://doi.org/10.1073/pnas.1910114117.

8. Xu et al., "Future of the Human Climate."

9. Matheus Gouvea de Andrade, "How Medellin Is Beating the Heat with Green Corridors," BBC, September 22, 2023, https://www.bbc.com/future/article/20230922-how-medellin-is-beating-the-heat-with-green-corridors.

10. Olga Khazan, "Why People Won't Stop Moving to the Sun Belt," *Atlantic*, August 15, 2023, https://www.theatlantic.com/ideas/archive/2023/08/moving-south-sun-belt-housing-economy/675010.

11. David A. Schkade and Daniel Kahneman, "Does Living in California Make People Happy? A Focusing Illusion in Judgments of Life Satisfaction," *Psychological Science* 9, no. 5 (1998): 340–6, https://doi.org/10.1111/1467-9280.00066.

12. Arthur Acolin and Vincent Reina, "Housing Cost Burden and Life Satisfaction," *Journal of Housing and the Built Environment* 37, no. 4 (2022): 1789–1815, https://doi.org/10.1007/s10901-021-09921-1.

13. Cigdem Gedikli et al., "The Relationship Between Unemployment and Wellbeing: An Updated Meta-Analysis of Longitudinal Evidence," *European Journal of Work and Organizational Psychology* 32, no. 1 (2023): 128–44, https://doi.org/10.1080/1359432X.2022.2106855.

14. Krekel and MacKerron, "How Environmental Quality."

15. Kati Orru et al., "Well-Being and Environmental Quality: Does Pollution Affect Life Satisfaction?" *Quality of Life Research* 25 (2016): 699–705, https://doi.org/10.1007/s11136-015-1104-6.

16. Marshall Burke et al., "The Changing Risk and Burden of Wildfire in the United States," *Proceedings of the National Academy of Sciences* 118, no. 2 (2021): e2011048118, https://doi.org/10.1073/pnas.2011048118.

17. Rebecca Lindsey, "Climate Change: Global Sea Level," Climate.gov, August 22, 2023, http://www.climate.gov/news-features/understanding-climate/climate-change-global-sea-level.

18. Krekel and MacKerron, "How Environmental Quality."

19. Sophie Knight, "What Would an Entirely Flood-Proof City Look Like?" *Guardian*, September 25, 2017, https://www.theguardian.com/cities/2017/sep/25/what-flood-proof-city-china-dhaka-houston.

20. Richard Schiffman, "He's Got a Plan for Cities That Flood: Stop Fighting the Water," *New York Times*, March 28, 2024, https://www.nytimes.com/2024/03/28/climate/sponge-cities-kongjian-yu.html.

21. Orru et al., "Well-Being and Environmental Quality."

22. Eric Klinenberg, "Adaptation," *New Yorker*, December 30, 2012, https://www.newyorker.com/magazine/2013/01/07/adaptation-eric-klinenberg.

23. Klinenberg, "Adaptation."

24. Jan C. Semenza et al., "Heat-Related Deaths During the July 1995 Heat Wave in Chicago," *New England Journal of Medicine* 335, no. 2 (1996): 84–90, https://doi.org/10.1056/NEJM199607113350203.

25. Arif Mohaimin Sadri et al., "The Role of Social Capital, Personal Networks, and Emergency Responders in Post-Disaster Recovery and Resilience: A Study of Rural Communities in Indiana," *Natural Hazards* 90, no. 3 (2018): 1377–1406, https://doi.org/10.1007/s11069-017-3103-0.

26. John F. Helliwell et al., "How Happy Are Your Neighbours? Variation in Life Satisfaction Among 1200 Canadian Neighbourhoods and Communities," *PLoS One* 14, no. 1 (2019): e0210091, https://doi.org/10.1371/journal.pone.0210091.

27. Adam Finnemann et al., "The Urban Desirability Paradox: U.K. Urban-Rural Differences in Well-Being, Social Satisfaction, and Economic Satisfaction," *Science Advances* 10, no. 29 (2024): eadn1636, https://doi.org/10.1126/sciadv.adn1636.

28. Sabrina Zwick, "Suburban Living the Worst for Carbon Emissions—New Research," United Nations University, July 19, 2021, https://unu.edu/article/suburban-living-worst-carbon-emissions-new-research.

29. "List of U.S. States by Renewable Electricity Production," Wikipedia, June 6, 2024, https://en.wikipedia.org/w/index.php?title=List_of_U.S._states_by_renewable_electricity_production&oldid=1227484661.

30. Liv Kelly, "The 19 Cities with the World's Best Public Transport—According to Locals," Time Out, March 20, 2025, https://www.timeout.com/travel/best-public-transport-in-the-world.

31. "Ranking 2024," TomTom, https://www.tomtom.com/traffic-index/ranking.

32. "10 Most and Least EV-Friendly Places to Live in America," iSeeCars, February 18, 2024, https://www.iseecars.com/ev-chargers-study.

33. Armando Quesada Webb, "Costa Rica's Green Energy Miracle Is at a Critical Juncture," *El País*, January 19, 2024, https://english.elpais.com/international/2024-01-19/costa-ricas-green-energy-miracle-is-at-a-critical-juncture.html.

34. "Change in CO_2 Emissions and GDP," Our World in Data, 2023, https://ourworldindata.org/grapher/co2-emissions-and-gdp?country=SWE~GBR~USA~FRA~DEU~OWID_EU27~CAN~CRI~OWID_ASI.

35. John F. Helliwell et al., "Statistical Appendix 1 for Chapter 2 of World Happiness Report 2021," in *World Happiness Report 2021* (Sustainable Development Solutions Network, 2021). https://files.worldhappiness.report/WHR21_Statistical_Appendix_01.pdf.

36. Helliwell et al., "How Happy Are Your Neighbours?"

37.   "Live, Work, and Explore in Costa Rica," Essential Costa Rica, https://www.visitcostarica.com/digital-nomads.

38.   Christian Krekel et al., "What Makes for a Good Job? Evidence Using Subjective Wellbeing Data," in *The Economics of Happiness: How the Easterlin Paradox Transformed Our Understanding of Well-Being and Progress*, ed. Mariano Rojas (Springer International, 2019), 241–68, https://doi.org/10.1007/978-3-030-15835-4_11.

39.   Krekel et al., "What Makes for a Good Job?"

40.   Krekel et al., "What Makes for a Good Job?"

41.   Alexander Pacek at al., "Well-Being and the Democratic State: How the Public Sector Promotes Human Happiness," *Social Indicators Research* 143, no. 3 (2019): 1147–59, https://doi.org/10.1007/s11205-018-2017-x.

42.   Rivka Liss-Levinson and Gerald Young, "State and Local Government Employees: Morale, Public Service Motivation, Financial Concerns, and Retention," MissionSquare Research Institute, March 6, 2023, https://research.missionsq.org/resources/state-and-local-government-employees-morale-public-service-motivation-financial-concerns-and-retention-2.

43.   Katie Kross, *Profession and Purpose: A Resource Guide for MBA Careers in Sustainability*, 2nd ed. (Routledge, 2017), https://doi.org/10.4324/9781351285841.

44.   Kross, *Profession and Purpose*.

45.   Michiko Namazu, "Saving Emissions with Sustainable Routing," Medium, June 9, 2023, https://medium.com/uber-under-the-hood/saving-emissions-with-sustainable-routing-e79fbec0962c.

46.   "Every Job Is a Climate Job," Kite Insights, https://kiteinsights.com/hubfs/Every-Job-Is-A-Climate-Job-Kite-Insights.pdf.

47.   Rachel Minkin et al., "The Experiences of U.S. Adults Who Don't Have Children," Pew Research Center, July 25, 2024, https://www.pewresearch.org/social-trends/2024/07/25/the-experiences-of-u-s-adults-who-dont-have-children.

48. Seth Wynes and Kimberly A. Nicholas, "The Climate Mitigation Gap: Education and Government Recommendations Miss the Most Effective Individual Actions," *Environmental Research Letters* 12, no. 7 (2017): 074024, https://doi.org/10.1088/1748-9326/aa7541.

49. Mikko Myrskylä and Rachel Margolis, "Happiness: Before and After the Kids," *Demography* 51, no. 5 (2014): 1843–66, https://doi.org/10.1007/s13524-014-0321-x.

50. Rachel Margolis and Mikko Myrskylä, "A Global Perspective on Happiness and Fertility," *Population and Development Review* 37, no. 1 (2011): 29–56, https://doi.org/10.1111/j.1728-4457.2011.00389.x.

51. Vivek H. Murthy, "Parents Under Pressure: The U.S. Surgeon General's Advisory on the Mental Health & Well-Being of Parents," US Department of Health and Human Services, August 14, 2024, https://www.hhs.gov/surgeongeneral/priorities/parents/index.html.

52. Jonathan Norman et al., "Comparing High and Low Residential Density: Life-Cycle Analysis of Energy Use and Greenhouse Gas Emissions," *Journal of Urban Planning and Development* 132, no. 1 (2006): 10–21, https://doi.org/10.1061/(ASCE)0733-9488(2006)132:1(10).

53. Phil Levin, "Babies @ Radish: The Early Review," *Supernuclear* (Substack), May 15, 2023, https://supernuclear.substack.com/p/babies-radish-the-early-review.

54. June McNicholas and Glyn M. Collis, "Dogs as Catalysts for Social Interactions: Robustness of the Effect," *British Journal of Psychology* 91, no. 1 (2000): 61–70, https://doi.org/10.1348/000712600161673.

55. Michael W. White et al., "Give a Dog a Bone: Spending Money on Pets Promotes Happiness," *Journal of Positive Psychology* 17, no. 4 (2022): 589–95, https://doi.org/10.1080/17439760.2021.1897871.

56. Wynes and Nicholas, "Climate Mitigation Gap."

57. Vivian Pedrinelli et al., "Environmental Impact of Diets for Dogs and Cats," *Scientific Reports* 12, no. 1 (2022): 18510, https://doi.org/10.1038/s41598-022-22631-0.

58. Xuefeng Peng et al., "The Effect of Pets on Happiness: A Large-Scale Multi-Factor Analysis Using Social Multimedia," *ACM Transactions on Intelligent Systems and Technology* 9, no. 5 (2018): 1–15, https://doi.org /10.1145/3200751.

CHAPTER 7. Upward Spirals of Joy

1. Bryan Bollinger and Kenneth Gillingham, "Peer Effects in the Diffusion of Solar Photovoltaic Panels," *Marketing Science* 31, no. 6 (2012): 900–12, https://doi.org/10.1287/mksc.1120.0727.

2. "Love & Climate—Hope & Noah," YouTube video, 4:52, posted by Green Jobs Board, August 26, 2024, https://www.youtube.com/watch?v=KZqj DRAOfQE.

3. Elisabeth Noelle-Neumann, "The Spiral of Silence: A Theory of Public Opinion," *Journal of Communication* 24, no. 2 (1974): 43–51, https://doi .org/10.1111/j.1460-2466.1974.tb00367.x.

4. Gregg Sparkman et al., "Americans Experience a False Social Reality by Underestimating Popular Climate Policy Support by Nearly Half," *Nature Communications* 13, no. 1 (2022): 4779, https://doi.org/10.1038 /s41467-022-32412-y.

5. Danielle F. Lawson et al., "Children Can Foster Climate Change Concern Among Their Parents," *Nature Climate Change* 9, no. 6 (2019): 458–62, https://doi.org/10.1038/s41558-019-0463-3.

6. Kenneth T. Gillingham and Bryan Bollinger, "Social Learning and Solar Photovoltaic Adoption," *Management Science* 67, no. 11 (2021): 7091–112, https://doi.org/10.1287/mnsc.2020.3840.

7. Gordon T. Kraft-Todd et al., "Credibility-Enhancing Displays Promote the Provision of Non-Normative Public Goods," *Nature* 563, no. 7730 (2018): 245–8, https://doi.org/10.1038/s41586-018-0647-4.

8. Edoardo M. Airoldi and Nicholas A. Christakis, "Induction of Social Contagion for Diverse Outcomes in Structured Experiments in Isolated

Villages," *Science* 384, no. 6695 (2024): eadi5147, https://doi.org/10.1126/science.adi5147.

9. Dominik Bentler et al., "Increasing Pro-Environmental Behavior in the Home and Work Contexts Through Cognitive Dissonance and Autonomy," *Frontiers in Psychology* 14 (2023), https://doi.org/10.3389/fpsyg.2023.1199363.

10. Andrew Prestwich et al., "Randomized Controlled Trial of Collaborative Implementation Intentions Targeting Working Adults' Physical Activity," *Health Psychology* 31, no. 4 (2012): 486–95, https://doi.org/10.1037/a0027672.

11. Felipe Kast at al., "Saving More in Groups: Field Experimental Evidence from Chile," *Journal of Development Economics* 133 (2018): 275–94, https://doi.org/10.1016/j.jdeveco.2018.01.006.

12. Cansu Ogulmus et al., "Social Contagion of Challenge-Seeking Behavior," *Journal of Experimental Psychology: General* 153, no. 10 (2024): 2573–87, https://doi.org/10.1037/xge0001620.

13. Bryan Bollinger et al., "Visibility and Peer Influence in Durable Good Adoption," *Marketing Science* 41, no. 3 (2022): 453–76, https://doi.org/10.1287/mksc.2021.1306.

14. Karen Hendricks, "How Pennsylvania Churches Are Addressing Climate Change by Tapping the Power of the Sun," StateImpact Pennsylvania, October 18, 2023, https://stateimpact.npr.org/pennsylvania/2023/10/18/how-pennsylvania-churches-are-addressing-climate-change-by-tapping-the-power-of-the-sun.

15. Jessica Schoner et al., "Is Bikesharing Contagious?: Modeling Its Effects on System Membership and General Population Cycling," *Transportation Research Record* 2587, no. 1 (2016): 125–32, https://doi.org/10.3141/2587-15.

16. Stefano Carattini et al., "Peer-to-Peer Solar and Social Rewards: Evidence from a Field Experiment," *Journal of Economic Behavior & Organization* 219 (March 2024): 340–70, https://doi.org/10.1016/j.jebo.2024.01.020.

17. Zakaria Babutsidze and Andreas Chai, "Look at Me Saving the Planet! The Imitation of Visible Green Behavior and Its Impact on the Climate Value-Action Gap," *Ecological Economics* 146 (April 2018): 290–303, https://doi.org/10.1016/j.ecolecon.2017.10.017.

18. James H. Fowler and Nicholas A. Christakis, "Dynamic Spread of Happiness in a Large Social Network: Longitudinal Analysis over 20 Years in the Framingham Heart Study," *BMJ* 337 (2008), https://doi.org/10.1136/bmj.a2338.

19. Cassie Flynn et al., *Peoples' Climate Vote 2024: Results* (UNDP, 2024), https://www.undp.org/publications/peoples-climate-vote-2024.

20. Elizabeth Dunn and Michael Norton, *Happy Money: The Science of Happier Spending* (Simon and Schuster, 2013).

21. Elizabeth M. Addonizio et al., "Putting the Party Back into Politics: An Experiment Testing Whether Election Day Festivals Increase Voter Turnout," *PS: Political Science & Politics* 40, no. 4 (2007): 721–7, https://doi.org/10.1017/S1049096507071168; and Ruairí Ó Cearúil et al., "Party at the Polls," When We All Vote, June 2023, https://whenweallvote.org/wp-content/uploads/2023/08/party-at-the-polls-2022.pdf.

22. Annika Stechemesser et al., "Climate Policies That Achieved Major Emission Reductions: Global Evidence from Two Decades," *Science* 385, no. 6711 (2024): 884–92, https://doi.org/10.1126/science.adl6547.

23. Abigail B. Sussman and Christopher Y. Olivola, "Axe the Tax: Taxes Are Disliked More Than Equivalent Costs," *Journal of Marketing Research* 48 (February 2011): S91–101, https://doi.org/10.1509/jmkr.48.SPL.S91.

24. Ryan J. Dwyer and Elizabeth W. Dunn, "Wealth Redistribution Promotes Happiness," *Proceedings of the National Academy of Sciences* 119, no. 46 (2022): e2211123119, https://doi.org/10.1073/pnas.2211123119.

25. Stechemesser et al., "Climate Policies That Achieved."

26. "En-ROADS Climate Scenario," Climate Interactive, November 2024, https://en-roads.climateinteractive.org/scenario.html.

27. "Sardine Feeding Frenzy with Sharks, Penguins and More | The Hunt | BBC Earth," YouTube video, 4:05, posted by BBC Earth, July 28, 2017, https://www.youtube.com/watch?v=6zOarcL1BSc.

28. Sara Brin Rosenthal et al., "Revealing the Hidden Networks of Interaction in Mobile Animal Groups Allows Prediction of Complex Behavioral Contagion," *Proceedings of the National Academy of Sciences* 112, no. 15 (2015): 4690–5, https://doi.org/10.1073/pnas.1420068112.

29. Damon Centola et al., "Experimental Evidence for Tipping Points in Social Convention," *Science* 360, no. 6393 (2018): 1116–9, https://doi.org/10.1126/science.aas8827.

30. "Al Gore on Climate Crisis: 'We Have the Solutions, but We've Got to Move Faster,'" Hubert H. Humphrey School of Public Affairs, October 29, 2021, https://www.hhh.umn.edu/research-centers/center-science-technology-and-environmental-policy/advancing-climate-solutions-now/speaker-al-gore.

INDEX

A Note About The Authors

Elizabeth Dunn is Professor of Psychology at the University of British Columbia and co-author of *Happy Money*. She directs UBC's Happy Lab, which focuses on how to optimize valuable resources including time, money, and carbon to maximize human well-being. Her work has been featured in the *New York Times*, BBC, *Washington Post*, *Los Angeles Times*, *The Atlantic*, *TIME*, *Rolling Stone* and *Harvard Business Review*; and on numerous podcasts and television shows. Dunn spoke on the TED mainstage in 2019, and her talk was selected as one of the top ten TED talks of the year.

Jiaying Zhao is Professor of Psychology and Sustainability and founded the Behavioral Sustainability Lab at the University of British Columbia. She has worked with NASA, NOAA, and the US and Canadian Forest Service to develop pathways to net zero. Zhao has appeared on numerous podcasts and in documentary films, including *Why Is This Happening? The Chris Hayes Podcast* and *Close the Divide*. Her research has been featured in the *New York Times, Washington Post, The Atlantic, TIME, The Economist, Scientific American,* CNN, and NBC. In 2023, Zhao gave a TED talk on climate strategies rooted in happiness, which was selected as one of the top TED Talks to be a better you in 2024.